A NEW LOOK
AT
Christmas Decorations

Happy American children share the joy
of decorating their own tree.

A NEW LOOK

AT

Christmas Decorations

ILLUSTRATIONS AND INSTRUCTIONS
by Sister M. Gratia Listaite, S.S.C., M.A.E.
Art Instructor
Maria High School, Chicago, Illinois

and

CUSTOMS AND TRADITIONS
by Norbert A. Hildebrand
Michigan State University
formerly with the Museum of Science and
Industry, Chicago, Illinois

THE BRUCE PUBLISHING COMPANY
MILWAUKEE

Library of Congress Catalog Card Number: 57–13320

© BY THE BRUCE PUBLISHING COMPANY
MADE IN THE UNITED STATES OF AMERICA

CHRISTMAS is often said to be for children. It were more truly said to be for the family. For this great holiday celebrating the birth of the Infant Jesus is also, in a sense, a feast of the Holy Family, bringing to mind, as it does, the blessings, trials, the joys, sorrows, and anxieties of Mary and Joseph. What mother does not kneel before the manger of Bethlehem pondering in her heart the miracle of birth? What father does not stand in kinship with Joseph as he recalls the fears and anxieties of providing for mother and Child? That little Family of the first Christmas is every man's family.

No wonder, then, that the traditions of Christmas in every land center upon the family and its symbols of security — the hearth and home. The special magic of Christmas is for everyone, and through its traditions and customs the bonds of family love are renewed and strengthened.

America itself is a family, a family of many nations and peoples whose different customs, languages, and cultures are still merging into a national character. And so, though the celebration of Christmas in our land varies widely from the snow-bound north to the sun-drenched south, Christmas itself remains a festival of the home, with the origin of its many varying customs in the family of nations. As each generation carries on with its particular family traditions, there takes place a further blending of the ethnic past, of quaint folklore and meaningful custom, with the ever evolving present. But the idea of the Christ Child remains the common denominator, so that for Americans there comes a new understanding of how our nation, from many, has become "one nation under God."

For many years Chicago's Museum of Science and Industry has presented at Christmas time a special program designed to recall the Christmas celebrations of other nations and to dramatize the contribution each of these nations has made to our own. In a series of programs called "Christmas Around the World" the Museum draws attention to the Christmas customs of other lands.

Out of the popularity of this program came the desire for a book that would help people to bring into their own Christmas celebrations the ideas of other nations, and would thus promote the feeling of national kinship.

To give practical expression to these contributions, the authors have made this a "do-it-yourself" book. The ideas were developed and worked out over a period of years by the art students of Maria High School in Chicago. The school is directed by the Sisters of Saint Casimir. All the art work was supervised by the instructor, Sister M. Gratia, S.S.C.

Furthermore, materials have been used that are readily at hand in most homes — drinking straws, colored paper, and the like. As a matter of fact, some of the projects are made from materials that are ordinarily thrown into the trash box or the rubbish burner.

In earlier days the family made its own Christmas decorations and gifts, and provided its own entertainment. Some of the things they made and did are recorded here. But in their new look at old decorations the authors felt that it would give added pleasure to adapt some of the old ideas to new materials. Thus, for example, instead of wheat straws for traditional Lithuanian tree ornaments, they have suggested that drinking straws be used. These preserve the spirit and the symbolism of the originals, but are actually a more practical material, and certainly more available.

Some liberty has also been taken in suggesting Christmas tree ideas for nations that have no tree tradition. Thus, for instance, in suggesting ideas for an Irish tree, the symbols ordinarily associated with the Irish — clay pipe, shamrock, leprechaun — are used.

This NEW LOOK AT CHRISTMAS DECORATIONS, then, attempts no more than to present a background of traditions and customs significant in our country's varied cultural inheritance, and to show how these ideas can be used in your own family celebration of Christmas.

ACKNOWLEDGMENTS

A NEW LOOK AT CHRISTMAS DECORATIONS was compiled and completed with the co-operation of many interested and help-giving persons. To all these I am deeply grateful for the time and practical suggestions accorded me in the course of this work.

Wholehearted gratitude is extended to my congregation, the Sisters of St. Casimir, for assisting me in this undertaking.

Sincerest thanks are especially due to all the art students at Maria High School, Chicago, for their assistance in making the ornaments and decorations depicted here. Most particularly am I indebted to Joan Zlotnik, art student, for her tireless and valuable contribution in assisting in the preparation of the art work in this volume.

Photographs featured in this book are predominantly by Donald Olson, of Chicago; other photographers are Vories Fisher and Anthony Comunale, also of Chicago.

— SISTER M. GRATIA LISTAITE, S.S.C.
Maria High School, Chicago

CONTENTS

Introduction	v
Acknowledgments	vi
THE CHRISTMAS TREE	1
UNITED STATES	2
GERMANY	6
WREATHS	12
CZECHOSLOVAKIA	13
HUNGARY	19
YUGOSLAVIA	21
SWITZERLAND	26
ITALY	30
CRÈCHE (PRAESEPIO)	35
SPAIN	42
MEXICO	50
FRANCE	55
BELGIUM	61
HOLLAND	65
ENGLAND-SCOTLAND	71
IRELAND	76
HOME DECORATIONS	80
NORWAY-SWEDEN	81
DENMARK	93
FINLAND	98
LITHUANIA	102
POLAND	111
UKRAINE	116
RUSSIA	120
GREECE	125
ARMENIA	129
CHINA-JAPAN	132
Reference Sources	146
Materials for Christmas Decorations	147
Discarded Material	148
Materials From Nature	149

ILLUSTRATIONS

UNITED STATES

Tree Detail	3
Bell Clusters	3
New England Lantern Pattern	4
Bell Pattern	5
Foil Flake Pattern	5

GERMANY

Tree	7
Dove Pattern	9
Bell Cluster Pattern	9
Tree Detail	10
Star and Straw Pattern	10
German Star Sketch	11

WREATHS

Advent Wreath	12
Wreath With Angel	12
Pin-Wheel Wreath	12

CZECHOSLOVAKIA

Tree	14
Tree Detail	15
Egg-Crate Dividers	15
Cherub Pattern	16
Egg-Crate Dividers Pattern	17
Paper Cup Pattern	17
Glorified Paper Cup	18

HUNGARY

Tree	20
Tree Detail	20

YUGOSLAVIA

Tree	22
Tree Detail	22
Tissue Garland and Basket	23
Paper Drinking Cup Basket	23
Tissue Paper Garland Sketch	24
Paper Mesh Basket Sketch	24
Angel Sketch	24
Streamlined Bird Pattern	25

SWITZERLAND

Tree	27
Tree Detail	28
Candy Basket Pattern	28
Pompom Snowbird Sketch	29
Alpine Hat Sketch	29

ITALY

Tree	31
Folded Star Sketch	32
3-D Star Sketch	32
Double Star Sketch	32
Snowflake Sketch	33
Star Construction	34

CRÈCHE (Praesipio)

Nativity Scene	36
Detail Crèche (A)	37
Crèche (A) Patterns	38
Crèche (B) Patterns	41

SPAIN

Spool Designs	42
Tree	43
Singing Spools	44
Cribs and Tambourines	44
Crib Shrine Sketch	45
Tambourine Sketch	45
Guitar Sketch	46
Fiddle Centerpiece	47
Magi	47
Magi Patterns	48
Magi Mosaic Panel	49

MEXICO

Tree	51
Tree Detail	51
Piñata Balls Sketch	52
Mexican Sombrero Pattern	53
Sombrero Window Pattern	54
Mexican Wrappings	54

FRANCE

Tree 56
Tree Detail 57
Cellophane Ball Sketch . . 57
Dancing Dolls . . . 58
Ballerina Centerpiece . . 58
French Ballerina Sketch . 59
Fleur-de-Lis Sketch . . 60

BELGIUM

Tree 61
Tree Detail . . . 62
Fluted Cup Bells . . 62
Bell Sketch . . . 62
Drum Sketch . . . 63
Accordion Sketch . . 63
Jolly Santa Pattern . . 64

HOLLAND

Tree Detail . . . 66
Dutch Duet Pattern . . 66
Windmill Pattern . . 67
Pin Wheel Pattern . . 67
Tree 68
Tulip 68
Sled Pattern . . . 69
Toy Windmill Sketch . . 69
Tulip Pattern . . . 70

ENGLAND-SCOTLAND

Tree 72
England Miniature Tree Pattern 73
3-D Flake Pattern . . . 73
Tree (Scotland) . . . 75

IRELAND

Tree 72
Tree Detail . . . 78
Irish Flower Sketch . . 78
Holiday Shamrock Pattern . 79
Clay Pipe Pattern . . 79
Home Decorations . . 80

NORWAY-SWEDEN

Santa Sleigh Reindeer . . 82
Reindeer Corner Decoration . 82
Styrofoam Birds . . 82
Reindeer Pattern . . 83

Tree (Spirit of Norway) . . 84
Yarn Doll Sketches . . 85
Mitten and Birdhouse Patterns 86
Tree (Sweden) . . . 87
Rooster and Cherub . . 88
Bird and Angel . . . 88
Goat and Straw Flower . . 88
Bird Pattern . . . 89
Cherub Pattern . . . 89
Straw Goat . . . 90
Straw Santa . . . 90
Rooster Sketches . . . 91
Goat Sketches . . . 92

DENMARK

Danish Basket . . . 93
Tree 94
Tree Detail . . . 94
Merry Mobile Sketch . . 95
Jul-Nisse Pattern . . 96
Danish Basket Pattern . 97

FINLAND

Tree 99
Tree Detail . . . 99
Finland's Fancies . . . 100
Baskets of Beauty Pattern . 101

LITHUANIA

Tree Detail . . . 102
Tree 103
Girls Making Ornaments . 104
Snowflake 105
Wayside Shrine . . . 105
Straw Dancer . . . 105
Geometric Ornament Sketch . 106
Straw Star Sketch . . 107
Family Trees . . . 108
Wonder Tree Pattern . . 109
Wonder Tree . . . 110
3-D Tree 110

POLAND

Tree Detail . . . 111
Peasant Angel Sketch . . 112
Eggshell Pitcher Pattern . 113
Porcupine Pattern . . . 113
Tree 114
Polish Designs . . . 115

UKRAINE

Tree Detail 117
Cherry Chain Pattern . . 117
Tree 118
Beaded Spider Sketch . . 119

RUSSIA

Tree 120
Tree Detail 121
Cossack Doll Pattern . . 122
Luminous Bird Pattern . . 123
Towers of Russia Sketch . 123
3-D Icon Pattern . . . 124

GREECE

Tree 126
Anchor Pattern . . . 126
Boat Pattern . . . 127
Angel Garland Pattern . 127
Boat Centerpiece . . . 128

ARMENIA

Tree 130
Tree Detail 130
Flights of Fancy Pattern . 131
Star (Baking Cup Liner) Sketch 131

CHINA-JAPAN

Chinese Pagoda Patterns . . 133
Airborne Pagoda Sketch . . 134
Jinrikisha Pattern . . . 135
Tree 136
Tree Detail 136
Jinrikisha 136
Oriental Butterfly Pattern . 137
Umbrella Sketch . . . 138
Japanese Fans 139
Japanese Tree 140
Stork Pattern 141

Polyethelyne Tubing Projects . 142
Scrap Sheet Metal Project . 142
Pine-Cone and Pipe-Cleaner
  Combination 143
Madonna and Angel Accents . 144
Packages 145

A NEW LOOK
AT
Christmas Decorations

THE CHRISTMAS TREE

THERE ARE MANY EXPLANATIONS, most of them legendary, concerning the origin of the Christmas tree. The fact that in pre-Christian times the evergreen was worshiped, used as a symbol of immortality, and because of its constant verdancy was thought to possess various magical properties, has complicated the problem of historical accuracy. Furthermore, aside from the specific idea of the Christmas tree, evergreen decorations in the home at Yule time have been popular among many central European peoples, from pre-Christian times.

But the Christmas tree as we think of it today originated rather late and stems from Christian, rather than pagan, tradition. Essentially, it comes from two medieval religious symbols — the Paradise tree and the Christmas light. In fact, in some countries — Italy, for example — the symbol of the "light" is still used and never did merge into a tree custom.

During medieval times, before the invention of movable type, when books were hand-written and too expensive and rare to be widely used, much religious teaching was provided through the medium of the drama. Religious plays, known as "miracle plays," were often performed in churches or on a rough platform in the church yard. They were called miracle plays because they depicted the miracles worked by Christ and the early saints. One of the most popular of these plays told the biblical story of creation, of Adam and Eve eating the forbidden fruit, and their expulsion from Paradise. The only stage decoration used was a fir tree, hung with apples, which represented the forbidden tree. Popularly, it became known as the "Paradise Tree." Because the play closed with the promise of the coming of Christ it was presented during the Advent season, as a means of preparing the faithful for Christmas.

In the fifteenth century, miracle plays were abandoned because of the abuses and irreverence which had crept in. But in continuing the observance of the feast day of Adam and Eve on December 24, people erected Paradise trees in their homes. Although the Roman Church never officially recognized sainthood for Adam and Eve, the Eastern Churches did, and the custom of observing this feast day came into Europe.

To December 24, Christmas Eve, belonged another religious custom — the Christmas light, symbolizing the birth of Christ as the Light of the World. In various countries it was customary to build a small pyramid-like frame, usually decorated with tinsel and glass balls, with a candle placed on top.

In Germany (about the 16th century) people began combining these two ideas — the fir tree with its apples was now given the tinsel and glass balls and the light on its top, and, to remind themselves that this was no longer a tree of sin, cookies and other good things were added to symbolize the religious significance of the "sweet fruit of Christ's salvation of mankind." The Christmas crib, formerly placed at the foot of the pyramid, now took its place under the tree, and the star candle of Bethlehem took the shape of a star at the treetop.

A German manuscript of 1605 is the first to mention this adaptation. From 1800 on, the idea spread swiftly throughout Europe and was brought to America by German immigrants.

Each country adopting the Christmas tree added its own ornament ideas to the fruit, glass balls, and tinsel with which it had started. Each addition involved some legendary or actual idea symbolizing man's homage to the newborn King. Though some of these ideas originated in superstition, they were not intended as an expression of such, but rather as a symbolization of the idea that the coming of the Christ Child meant an end to the darkness of pre-Christian beliefs.

THE UNITED STATES

THE CHRISTMAS TREE came to America from Germany. The first decorated trees in the country were those set up by homesick Hessian troops during the Revolutionary War. But it was many years before the custom itself began.

One of the first known trees was set up by Charles Follen, a German professor at Harvard, in 1832. Another is credited to August Imgard of Wooster, Ohio, who as a recent arrival from Germany, decorated a tree for his nephew and niece in 1847.

Cleveland, Ohio, had a tree in 1851, set up by Pastor Henry Schwan for his congregation. When some of his people objected to it as a pagan practice, the religious character of its origin was explained, and the objections were dropped.

President Franklin Pierce did much to spread the custom by having a Christmas tree in the White House (1850's) when the Sunday school of the New York Avenue Presbyterian church was entertained there. President Benjamin Harrison continued the practice and soon the Christmas tree became an American tradition.

It was another American president, however, who almost stopped the custom. President Theodore Roosevelt, noted for his efforts in the conservation of our natural resources, banned the Christmas tree tradition at the White House. His sons, however, smuggled a tree in and, when confronted with their crime, were defended by America's first forester, Gifford Pinchot. Pinchot convinced the president that the cutting of young evergreens could be helpful in forest conservation and in so doing established a new industry in America, which now annually markets some twenty million Christmas trees. Today's trees come largely from the northern forests of our country, from Canada, and in recent years from tree plantations where special varieties are cultivated exclusively for the Christmas tree market.

Christmas tree ornaments in the United States come from all over the world in the sense that each nationality has brought its own decoration ideas to its new home. In the early days, decorations were simple and home made, fashioned of the things common to our agricultural past. Apples were plentiful and oranges were a special treat before transportation and refrigeration solved the seasonal problem. Nuts, popcorn balls, cranberry strings, and paper ornaments were the rule until German imported ornaments became popular. These came largely from the Thuringian mountain region of Germany where whole families worked the year round in preparing for the seasonal trade. Japan also came into the market.

The scarcity of ornaments during World War II prompted American production and today many of our ornaments come from Wellsboro, Pennsylvania, and the Corning Glass Company.

One of the most important contributions to the Christmas tree is the American invention of electric lights. Today, thanks to Thomas Edison, we can enjoy the Christmas tree in a multitude of colored lights, without the tragedies that marked so many homes when candles were in use.

The use of tree lights for outdoor decorations is another American contribution to the holiday atmosphere. All over the country, this custom of decorating front yards, windows, and homes with lights has become popular, and entire communities are now lighted by such decorative displays for the season.

Along with such individual home decorations, the community Christmas tree, erected in some central spot, is becoming almost universal as a part of Christmas programming.

"One Nation under God, Indivisible, with Liberty and Justice for all."

Glittering foil flakes and bells may also be used for window and door decorations.

In creating more unusual effects, Americans have also initiated the idea of spraying whole trees with various colored materials. No longer need trees be naturally green — today one has a choice of silver, gold, pink, blue, and almost any color desired — even black. But the simplicity of the traditional tree in its natural state will always be attractive.

Another American contribution to Christmas is the personification of Santa Claus. Though he originated in the folklore of other countries (his conception came from the pagan Germanic god, Thor), it was an American — Dr. Clement C. Moore of New York — who in 1822 wrote the famous poem, "A Visit from St. Nicholas." Dr. Moore's reference to St. Nicholas was based on a Dutch tradition — still observed in many countries — honoring a benevolent saint of the early centuries. The Dutch name for St. Nicholas was "Sinter Klaas" which became our Santa Claus, but the characterization of face and dress came from the mythical Thor who drove a chariot pulled by two white goats called "Cracker and Gnasher."

Thus two folk legends and a small pinch of history were combined by Dr. Moore in his well-loved poem which was first published in the Troy, New York, *Sentinel* in 1823. Then the famous cartoonist, Thomas Nast, pictured Santa Claus in *Harper's Illustrated Weekly* in 1863, and for his illustration drew on his childhood memories of Germany and "Pelze Nichol" who brought children presents.

Thus was born the Santa Claus of our day.

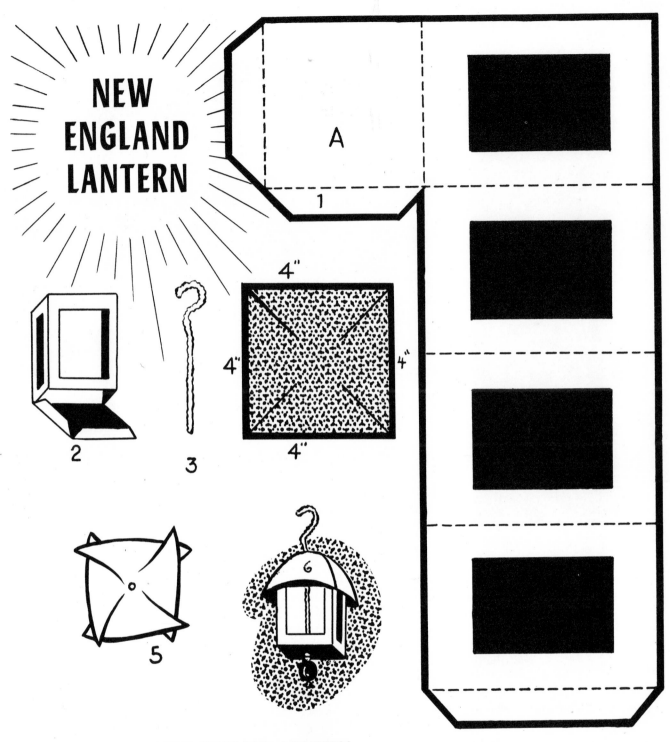

NEW ENGLAND LANTERN

1. Trace and cut Fig. A from red mat stock. Fold on dotted lines.
2. Fold bottom flaps up and glue them in place.
3. Shape hook from pipe cleaner.
4. Make a 4-in. square (roof) of same material used in Fig. A. Draw diagonal lines from all corners, stopping within ½ in. of the center.
5. Overlap flaps of roof, then staple and cut off projecting tabs. Make holes in roof and base.
6. Insert pipe cleaner through holes in roof and base. Attach a colored bead or gummed circle to bottom of pipe cleaner.

BELLS

FOIL FLAKES

BELLS

1. For one cluster of bells, trace seven metallic circles of any desirable size.
2. Fold circle in half. Fringe edges. Form a cone and staple in place. Knot the end of a long string and slide one bell on string until stopped by knot. Repeat *step 2*, spacing bells evenly. Arrange three bells on one side of string and four on the other when suspending on branch. Colored beads may be strung between bells.

FOIL FLAKES

1. Cut a strip of metallic paper 22 in. long and 2½ in. wide.
2. Fold paper into ½-in. pleats.
3. Cut angular designs on folded paper.
4. Run a threaded needle through each fold ½ in. from bottom.
5. Tie pleats together loosely. Join open ends with glue or staples.

5

GERMANY

"FROEHLICHE WEINACHTEN"

MUCH of the world's Christmas tradition is of Germanic origin — not necessarily from the geographical Germany of recent times, but from the vast forested areas of the central European heartland, where various tribes successively left their imprint on the land and in the legends of the area.

Western civilization first came into contact with these Germanic tribes when they were partly conquered by the Roman legions of Julius Caesar in 58 B.C., but not until about A.D. 700 and St. Boniface, the Apostle of Germany, did Christianity gain a hold on the area. The German nation as such did not emerge until the reign of Charlemagne in A.D. 800.

As a result of this intermingling of ethnical and religious culture of Germanic and Roman paganism, and finally Christianity, superstitious custom and Christian practice were likewise intermingled. Much of the paganism of this pre-Christian era survives in the Christmas traditions of today.

The most significant of these pagan customs was the celebration of the winter solstice, which marked the end of the shortening hours of daylight and the beginning of the sun's apparent return to the earth. It is this festival which gives us the word "Yule" to mark this season of the year.

Fire played an important part in the ritual of this observance in honor of Hertha or Bertha, the goddess of the home. Evergreens decorated the home and a great altar of flat stones was erected on which a fire of fir boughs was built. It was believed that Hertha descended through the smoke, and at the feast which followed the priests would forecast the future of those assembled. Everyone then took a part of the sacred fire to kindle a Yule log on his own hearth, a log which must be completely burned lest misfortune follow.

In some areas, it was Thor, the god of the peasants or common people, who was so honored. He was represented as an old man, with a long white beard, who was friendly to people. He could be heard roaring through the heavens in his golden chariot drawn by two white goats (Cracker and Gnasher) in the thunder of a rainstorm. The lightning, a firebolt he threw, was his power, and his color was red. He lived in the far north, among the icebergs, and he fought the gods of ice and snow, thus helping humans in an annual conquest of the most feared season of the year, when darkness and cold held the earth in thrall.

From these mythological concepts and the customs attending the solstice celebration have come many of the traditions of Europe — the ceremonial burning of the Yule log and games of fortunetelling, and the characterization of Santa Claus as he is known in America.

The god Thor first became Father Christmas in early Germany and in that guise retained his benevolent role which was indicated by the gifts he brought for children.

With the coming of Christianity, a new figure captured the imagination of the people. This was St. Nicholas, a fourth-century bishop of Myra in Asia Minor. He was known for his miracles and for his generosity, for he was born of wealth but gave it to the poor and dedicated his life to God. Many stories were told of his miracles — once he calmed the sea with his prayers when a

6

CONTINUED ON PAGE 8.

"Tree of Paradise" lit with stars and candles.

CONTINUED FROM PAGE 6.

storm threatened to wreck the ship he was on, and he became the patron saint of sailors as a result. Again he was instrumental in saving his province from starvation when he persuaded captains of the imperial grain ships to let him have a part of their cargo. When the ships arrived at their destination in Constantinople the grain was miraculously increased to its original quantity, thus saving the captains from punishment for their generosity.

Another miracle attributed to him concerns the restoration to life of three boys who had been killed and robbed by an innkeeper whom St. Nicholas forced to confess his crimes. Thus he became the patron saint of children.

One of the most popular legends of the good saint's deeds concerns the dowry he provided for three daughters of a poor nobleman, who without such wealth would have had little chance for marriage. His gifts, a bag of gold, left secretly in the night for each girl as she became old enough for marriage, established him as the patron saint of maidens looking for a husband. And the symbol of his generosity, three bags of gold, became three balls which were first adopted by bankers in Italy as a symbol of St. Nicholas, their patron saint. Later this sign became associated with pawnbrokers and is still used today.

Because he was said to have been made a bishop while rather young, St. Nicholas was known as the "Boy Bishop," and it later became customary in many parts of Europe to honor him by having a youth, dressed in the robes of a bishop, lead a procession to the church on his feast day.

In Germany, the feast of St. Nicholas was celebrated on December 6, and he was represented as riding a white horse and accompanied by his servant Rupprecht, a thin, dark man carrying a sack in which to put bad children. St. Nicholas, of course, carried gifts for the good children. (The custom of hanging up stockings is said to have originated from the story about St. Nicholas' gift of a bag of gold to one of the dowerless daughters, which accidentally fell into a stocking hung near the chimney to dry.)

When a large part of Germany, moved by the teachings of Martin Luther, separated from the Roman Catholic Church, St. Nicholas was replaced by "Kris Kringle," who was depicted as a young girl wearing a golden crown and carrying a small Christmas tree, "the tree of light." Kris Kringle was considered a messenger from the Christkind, or Christ Child, and personified the idea of gift giving.

From this varied background, German Christmas tree ornaments take many different forms including the bearded face and peaked cap of Father Thor, the representations of St. Nicholas as a bishop, and the golden-haired angel girl, Kris Kringle. Apples and oranges come from the miracle plays of medieval days when the evergreen tree, representing the "tree of paradise," was hung with the "forbidden fruit" to symbolize the temptation of Adam and Eve in the Garden of Eden.

The various ball ornaments are the bags of gold of St. Nicholas.

To these things were added the hand-carved animals and birds which legend recounted as worshiping at the stable in Bethlehem, the little toys German wood carvers made for their sons and daughters at Christmas, and the paper stars and angels representing the heralds of Christ's birth. These are the things we think of today as the wonderful old-fashioned ornaments of our childhood when German importations were at their peak.

Our new version of these German ornaments, formerly made of blown glass, include representations of many of these old ideas.

8

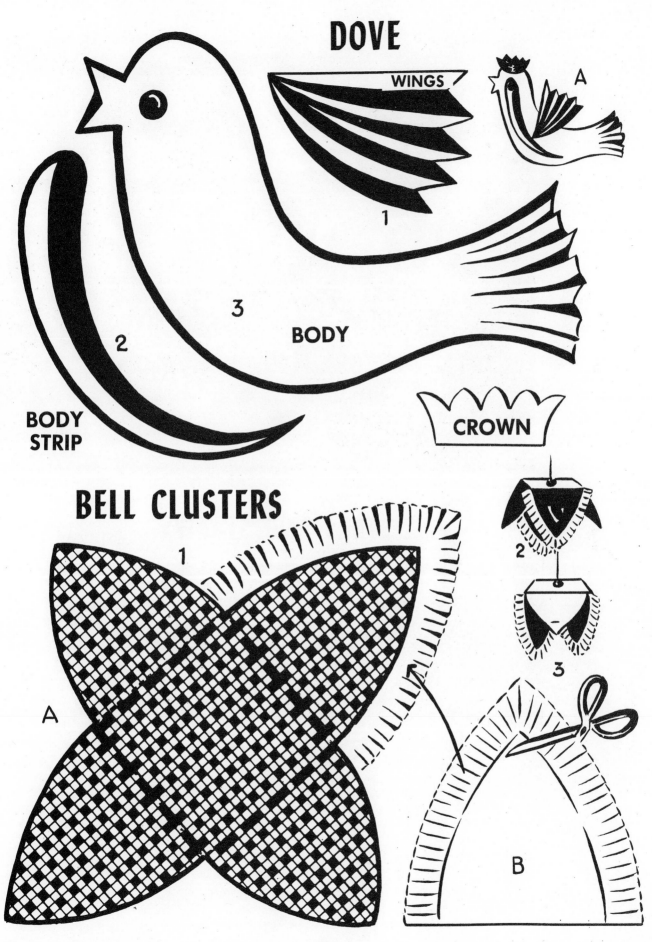

DOVE

WINGS

A

1

BODY

3

BODY
STRIP

2

CROWN

2

3

BELL CLUSTERS

1

A

B

9

New ideas born of old memories.

STARS AND STRAWS

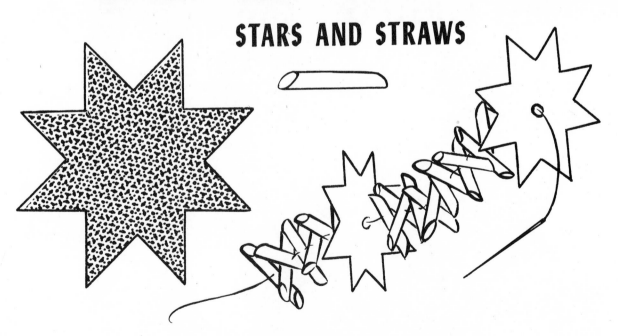

STARS AND STRAWS

1. Make stars from colored construction paper, using many colors, if possible.
2. Cut drinking straws 1½ in. long.
3. Insert one large star after every 12 straw segments.

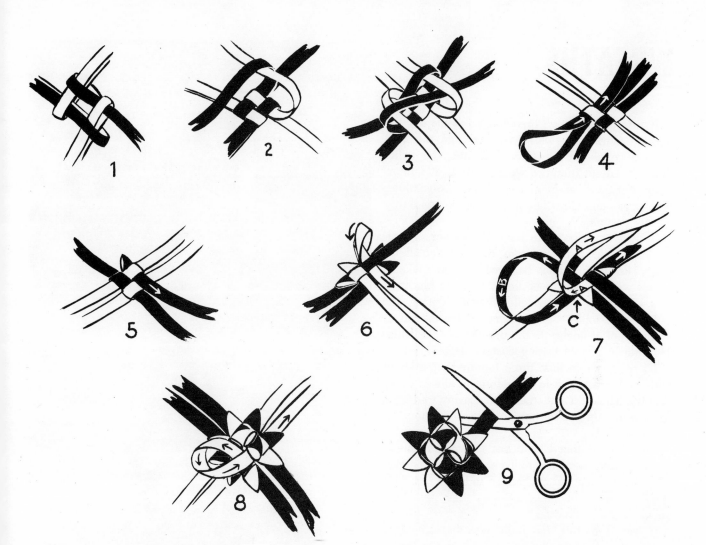

GERMAN STAR

1. Fold four pieces of ribbon or paper, two light and two dark, in half. (Make each ¾ by 24 in.) Interlock to form basket weave and pull ends tightly.
2. Lift top ribbons; fold one across the other to form second basket weave.
3. Pull ends tightly.
4. Bring one loose end up and slip it through one open side. Turn loop inside out with thumb and forefinger.
5. Pull end through until loop forms point or triangle when creased (see diagram). Repeat with remaining three loose ends. Now you have four star points.
6. Turn star over and repeat *steps 4* and *5*. Now there are eight star points.
7. To make center standing points, lift and fold back one of the top light-colored strips (A). Take dark strip (B); keeping the right side up, loop the strip counterclockwise and slip it into slot (C) under raised ribbon. Pull through to form a point at (C).

8. Repeat procedure with remaining top strips to make four standing points. Turn star over and repeat *steps 7* and *8*.
9. Trim extending ribbons.

DOVE

1. Trace: one body, two crowns, two wings, and two body strips.
2. Crease wings and body strips as shown in *patterns 1* and *2*.
3. Glue pieces in place on both sides of body (see Fig. A).

BELL CLUSTERS

1. Trace one pattern of A and two of B. Glue the fringed flaps to reverse side of two large flaps of *pattern A* (see arrow and Fig. 2).
2. Fold all flaps down on dotted lines.
3. Staple smaller flaps together at lowest point. String and suspend.

WREATHS

THE use of evergreen branches for home decorations at Christmas stems basically from the Yule observance of pre-Christian days and the belief that its verdant qualities were symbols of immortality. But there are many legends and associations, both pagan and Christian, to explain the popularity of this custom.

Holly was believed to have the power of protection — from witches, from thunder and lightning. The burning bush from which God spoke to Moses was thought to be holly. In some places, it was customary to reconcile enemies during the Yule season under the branches of the holly tree, as a symbol of fidelity to the promise of friendship. Thus the mistletoe kissing custom started.

There are more than three hundred varieties of holly and it is found in some form in almost every country. Thus it is not strange that many traditions have grown up from primitive times regarding this unusual plant.

One story is that Christ was crowned with the thorny branches of the holly and that its berries, which were then white, changed to blood red. This story served early missionaries in their preaching on the Lord's sufferings.

It was from this that holly wreaths came into popularity and a candle was placed in the center to remind people of the new Light of the World that was born on Christmas day.

From this came another custom which began in Germany a few hundred years ago with the Lutheran Church. This is the Advent wreath, which may consist simply of a wreath of holly with four candles placed in the center to represent the four weeks of Advent.

"Advent" means *coming* — specifically the coming of Christ — thus the four weeks of Advent are meant as a spiritual preparation for commemorating the birth of Christ. On each of the four Sundays before Christmas a candle of the Advent wreath is lighted while the family joins in prayer. Its symbolism is to remind the faithful of the Old Testament, when mankind lived in fear and darkness awaiting the coming of the Saviour.

The wreath itself is an early symbol of victory and glory; thus when the four candles are lit on the last Sunday before Christmas, the time is at hand when the Lord shall be born and, as the Light of the World, fulfill the promise of the Old Testament.

"VESELE VANOCE"

IN CZECHOSLOVAKIA the Christmas season begins on December 6 with Svaty Mikulas day and ends with Tri Kralu on January 6, that is, from St. Nicholas day to the feast of the Three Kings.

For the children it is St. Nicholas who brings the presents but there is always some question as to whether his visit will mean reward or punishment — at least in theory. For accompanying St. Nicholas, who descends from heaven on a golden cord, are an angel dressed in white and a devil known as Cert who is dressed in black. Cert carries a whip and rattles a chain so, as the group makes its customary rounds, the rattle of the chain can be heard.

This is a signal for the good little boys and girls to say their prayers and, if they know them well, the good angel will leave an appropriate gift. If on the contrary, the prayers don't go well, old Cert will be ready with his whip.

The season is typical of the Christmas season everywhere. There is the caroling in the streets and in the homes, and dancing and eating following the fasting, which ends on Christmas eve. Friends and neighbors and relatives are constantly visiting and it is customary for all those who have quarreled during the year to forgive each other publicly.

Carolers carrying miniature Bethlehem scenes go from house to house giving informal concerts after which they must be invited in for a glass of wine and a sample of "Vanocka," a sweet roll filled with raisins and almonds.

Little boys, dressed as the Three Kings, also sing for their treats.

In former days, and probably in many Czech homes today, party fun was of the homespun variety and many of the games and customs were directed at pairing off the young people properly. Christmas fun everywhere seems to be especially directed at matchmaking efforts, and probably grew out of the necessity of making hay while the sun shone or rather while the sun wasn't shining. For the Christmas holiday in any agricultural environment is the only time of the year when the work of tilling the soil and caring for the livestock comes to a pause — it has always been a time when farmers can relax and enjoy social festivities. Thus it is little wonder that the young girls had a variety of schemes to get the young men of their fancy in the mood for marriage.

They also had special ways of forecasting their expected betrothal.

For example, little boats were made of the halves of walnut shells. These were floated, each with a lit candle, in a tub of water. The girl whose candle burned the longest could expect to be married during the coming year.

Again, from a pile of kindling for the fire, each girl would draw a stick. A long stick meant a tall husband, a thick one indicated a stout one, a short stick, a small man, and so on. By dropping melted lead into a pan of water, his occupation could be foretold from the shape of the lead as it cooled. Since there weren't too many occupations to choose from it was fairly simple to interpret these lead shapes into something coincidental with the man already marked for marriage.

The Czech Christmas tree had a variety of ornaments, especially representations of the angels who accompanied St. Nicholas. Gaily colored pinwheels, suspended by thread, looked like multicolored jewels or falling snowflakes and twinkling stars. Gilded walnuts also provided boats for the party games, and a variety of bells, hung in clusters of three, four, or five on bright ribbons, were popular. Eggshells also made a variety of ornaments, either decorated or used to make the bodies of strange-looking fish.

A
Czechoslovakian
fantasy.

Fruits of the imagination.

From egg crate dividers to holiday trimmings.

15

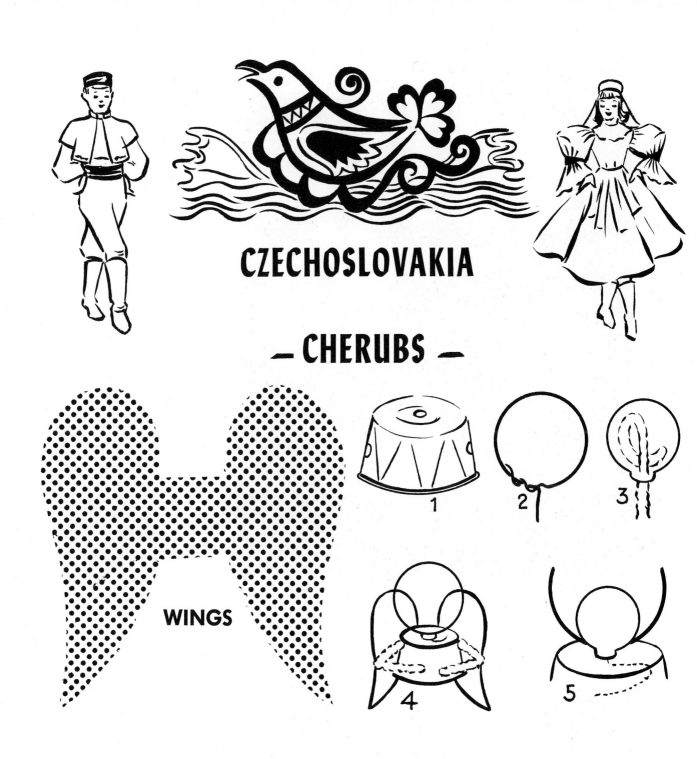

CZECHOSLOVAKIA

— CHERUBS —

WINGS

CHERUB

1. Punch a hole on the top and one on each side of an inverted paper salad cup.
2. With a white pipe cleaner, form halo 2½ in. in diameter.
3. For head, insert pipe cleaner into a Christmas ball.
4. For arms, insert another pipe cleaner through side holes in cup. Insert halo through top hole of cup and tape pipe cleaner inside cup. Trace pattern of wings; glue or staple these to back of cup.
5. Insert head through top hole and tape pipe cleaner in place.

FANTASTIC FLOWERS
OF
CZECHOSLOVAKIA

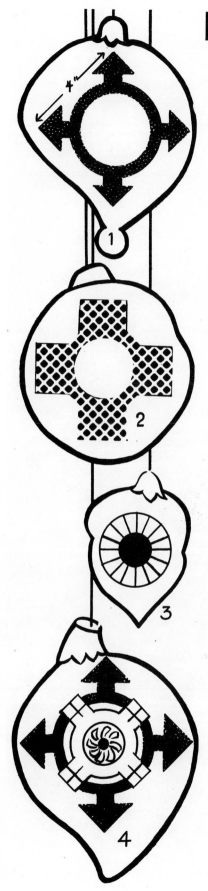

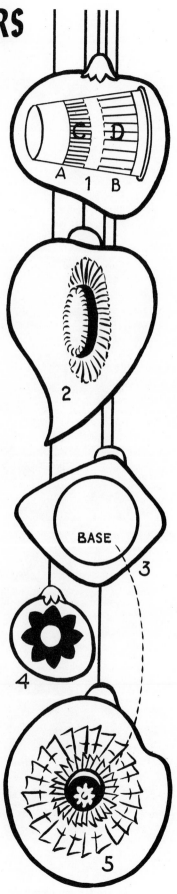

EGG CRATE DIVIDERS
(Left)

1. Enlarge *pattern 1* at left to 4 in. Use heavy paper.
2. Cut out section of egg crate divider and paint.
3. Make a yellow circle 2 in. in diameter and attach small red circle to center of it. Make slits in circle as far as red center and bend every other slit toward center.
4. Glue No. 2 on No. 1 and No. 3 on No. 2. Decorate with glitter (Fig. 4).

PAPER CUP
(Right)

1. Cut off top and bottom of a paper cup (see lines *A* and *B*).
2. Cut in on *C* and *D* lines. Bend fringed edges outward.
3. For base of ornament, make a circle 3½ in. in diameter.
4. Trace pattern of bud.
5. Glue fringed piece to base and bud to center of fringe.

Paper cups are transformed into a delightful cluster of silent bells.

"BOLDOG KARACSONY"

THE early history of Hungary is a succession of migratory waves which began with the Magyars, a nomadic tribe from the East, and ended with the Germans from the West. Agriculture replaced their nomadic existence and Christianity their heathenism with the reign of King Stephen in the tenth century.

Thus the Christmas traditions of central Europe, and particularly those of Germany, merged with Eastern pagan customs. But even then the turmoil did not end. There was physical conquest from the Turks and later from Austria. There was also religious strife, with consequent changing beliefs, in the various sections of the country.

As a result, Hungary, even in the matter of Christmas customs, was a mixture of many things.

In some areas, St. Lucia's day, December 13, was the beginning of the Christmas season and, to mark the occasion, groups of boys chanting religious songs would visit the farm homes. It was believed that the fertility of hens and geese would be assured by this custom. In return the boys were rewarded with cake and cookies.

The German Kris Kringle was also known in Hungary, but here as a male, dressed in white, who made his rounds on a white horse. Cookies were popularly baked in the shape of horseshoes in his honor, and they were filled with poppy seeds (an Eastern influence) or walnuts. There was also a fudge candy that was made especially for the Christmas season.

In other respects, Christmas was observed in Hungary much in the same way as among her neighbors to the west.

Christmas Eve ended the days of fasting and it was customary at the evening meal to set an extra place at table for the stranger who might knock at the door in search of hospitality.

Family visits and family parties were typical and there were many varieties of fortunetelling stunts to liven these occasions. Crumbs swept from the floor after the Christmas Eve supper were to be thrown across the threshold at midnight by the girl in search of a husband, and her future spouse's face would appear to her as she threw. This worked quite well when the young man who was so inclined happened to stop by to escort the young lady to midnight Mass.

A bowl of water set outside the house to freeze on Christmas Eve also indicated by the pattern in the ice the future husband's occupation.

Cutting an apple in two indicated the health of the person for the coming year. If the pattern (as cut through the middle) was a regular, star-shaped one, it meant good health. If the pattern was broken, sickness would follow.

Ashes from the Yule log, when placed at the foot of fruit trees, insured a bountiful harvest.

With such accent on agricultural magic, it is natural to find the Hungarian Christmas tree decorations indicating similar ideas — nuts, cookies, and paper cornucopia filled with Szalon Cukor, the Christmas fudge. Popcorn strings and other edibles completed the tree trimmings to which were added decorated cards bearing Christmas messages — and often a verse of good fortune.

Popcorn garlands
give this tree
a tasty look.

"SRETAN BOZIC"

SINCE prehistoric times, fire has meant home and security to man. Its heat cooked his meat and warmed him, and its light protected him from marauding animals and the terrors of darkness. And even today, when man has learned to make fire in new ways, to control and confine its use in the home in more efficient though less picturesque methods than his ancestors, the family hearth still retains its ancient enchantment. Thus it is little wonder that fire was once worshiped by men who created many forms of ritual in its honor.

The Yule log was part of that ritual, and so dominant was its role that even though Christianity dispelled the darkness of the ignorance in which it once flourished, its tradition is still observed today.

Before the coming of Christianity man built his sacred fires to his heathen gods and, during the winter solstice, when the cold, dark nights of winter were longest, when the life-giving sun seemed to have deserted the earth and left man in the clutches of the ice giants, then his sacred fires burned most fiercely. This began the Yule log.

For the Druids, it had to be the trunk of a fruit-bearing tree like the apple. For the Germanic nations it was the fir. For others it was the oak, the ash, or the birch. But always it was a large tree, a trunk, for in the earliest tradition it represented the "tree of the universe," a tree so large no human could think of it, with one root in heaven and the other in hell, and the third in the earth, while at its feet gnawed the creatures of darkness.

The Yule log was often selected months in advance so it could be felled and allowed to dry out thoroughly before the ritual of its burning began. But in Yugoslavia it was not cut until the dawn of Christmas when the young men of the family would search the forests for a strong young oak for the "Badnjak." It must fall toward the east at the exact moment of sunrise and its branches must not touch those of surrounding trees. It must be large enough to burn throughout the Christmas season, for if its fire should go out, tragedy would surely fall upon the household.

All who helped bring in the Yule log were safe from witchcraft during the year, so the whole family participated in the effort.

Once the log was burning brightly on the hearth, the family gathered around its cheerful warmth to listen to the stories about its magical properties and to await the coming of "Polaznik," a young man selected for the role of the first visitor to enter the house on Christmas morning.

First Polaznik must throw a handful of grain at each member of the family and ask a blessing on the household. Then the log was struck and the number of sparks which flew up indicated the number of sheep, cattle, and pigs which were to be born in the coming year.

Next, wine was poured on the log as a token of thanksgiving for the harvest gathered. Polaznik then left a silver coin on one end of the log to assure the family of food and fortune throughout the year.

The Yugoslavian Christmas tree is distinguished particularly by the many angels in its decoration. For angels have an important duty to perform on Christmas Eve. As they proclaim the birth of the Infant King, they dip their wings in the village springs and thus purify the water.

At dawn the maidens fill their pitchers with this angel-blessed water to be drunk on Christmas day. A handful of corn and a sprig of basil are then thrown into the spring to safeguard the water's purity and insure a good harvest.

YUGOSLAVIA

Striking paper-cup angels,
delicate weblike baskets,
and chains add a bit of heaven
to the Yugoslavian tree.

22

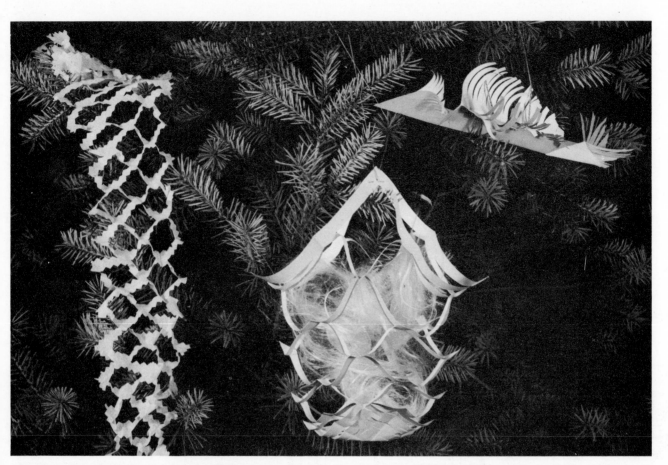

Colorful paper birds bring nature indoors.

Tiny angelic choirs herald the arrival of Christmas.

TISSUE-PAPER GARLANDS

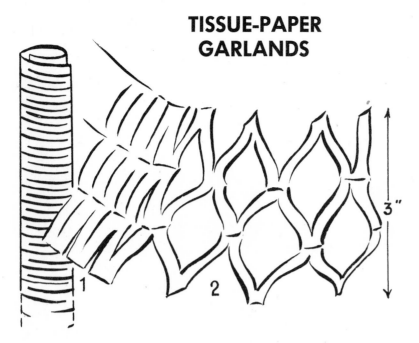

TISSUE-PAPER GARLANDS

1. Take a strip of white tissue paper 3 in. wide and any desired length. Fold paper vertically into thirds. Alternate slits as in Figure 1.
2. Open and pull carefully.

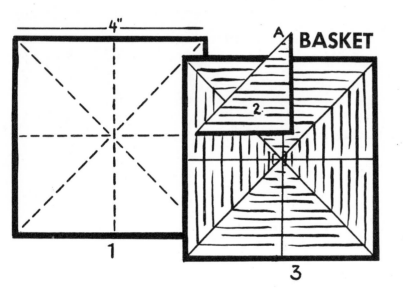

PAPER MESH BASKET

1. Fold 4-in. square in half twice, then fold diagonally (see Fig. 1).
2. Find center of original square (point A) and begin making alternate slits (Fig. 2).
3. Reopen to original square. Pull center down to form the basket. See photograph.

ANGEL

1. Cut off the tip of a paper drinking cup (Fig. A). One fifth of the way down punch a hole on each side of cup. For arms, insert pipe cleaner through the two side holes. Bend and form arms. Fasten a Christmas ball on wooden bead into the open part (see Fig. A).
2. Make wings from cupcake liner by snipping out section from top and bottom.
3. Insert halo made of wire or pipe cleaner into neck hole behind head. Pin wings to back. Decorate body of angel with glitter.

YUGOSLAVIA

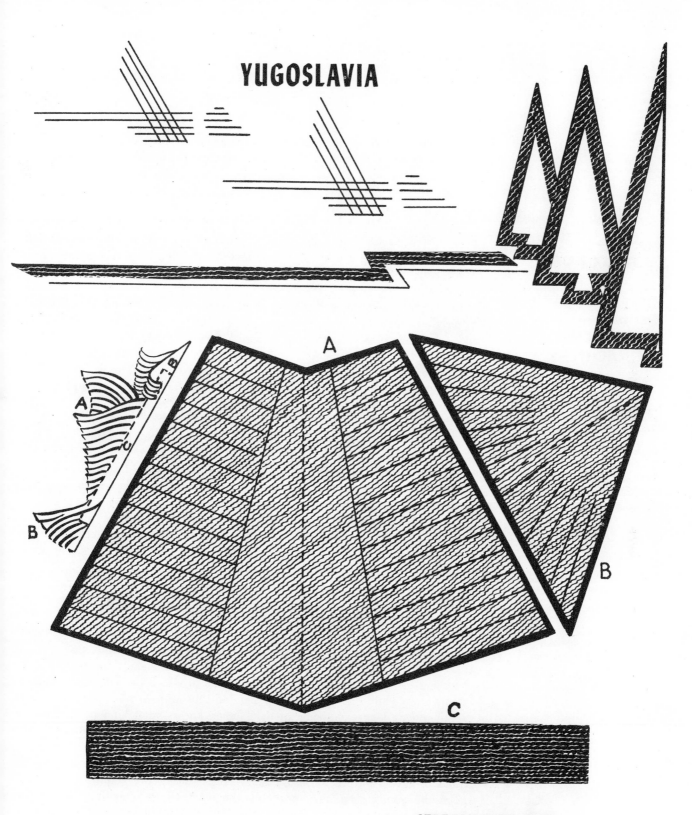

STREAMLINED BIRD

1. Trace *patterns A* (wings) and *C* (body base) once, and *pattern B* (head and tail) twice on colored construction paper. Fringe head, tail, and wings. Fold on dotted lines.
2. Glue head, wings, and tail to body base. Curl fringe with any metal instrument.

SWITZERLAND

French —
"JOYEUX NOEL"

German —
"FROEHLICHE WEINACHTEN"

Italian —
"BONO NATALE"

AS INDICATED by the greetings exchanged in Switzerland at Christmas time, the cultures of many nations have been merged in this tiny country.

The international flavor of its languages is duplicated in its Christmas traditions.

In most parts of Switzerland, the tradition of St. Nicholas is observed, but with variations. He arrives on December 6, and, as elsewhere, distributes candy, fruit, and toys. Sometimes a parade is held in his honor, with a giant figure of St. Nicholas leading a group of youngsters dressed in long white night-gowns and wearing masks. Accompanied by the blowing of the long Swiss horns and by bells, the paraders solicit toys and fruit along the way, which are then later distributed among them.

In regions observing a variation of this custom, it is "Samichlaus" who is eagerly awaited by the youngsters on the eve of December 5. Wearing a red, laughing mask, fur-trimmed robes, a flowing white beard, and carrying a large well-stuffed sack and a staff to support him, Samichlaus starts his gift distribution with a procession from the village church. He is preceded by boys wearing high-peaked snow hoods and robes, carrying a cross and banners, along with the church choir and clergy singing Christmas songs.

In other villages the gift bringer is "Father Christmas" and his wife, Lucy, who visit the children. Lucy comes from the Scandinavian tradition (St. Lucy's feast day is December 13). Father Christmas wears the traditional white beard and fur-trimmed robe and brings gifts for the boys, while Lucy, with a round white cap over her braids, and dressed in a silk gown and laced bodice, brings presents for the girls.

These variations of St. Nicholas have also been replaced in some parts of Switzerland with the Christkind or "Christ Child" who travels across the land in the tradition of America's Santa Claus, with a large, well-stocked sleigh drawn by six reindeer.

In the rural areas, many folk traditions associated with the Christmas season are popular.

A grandmother, for example, selects a perfect onion on the night before Christmas, and cutting it in half, peels off twelve layers — one for each month of the coming year. These peelings are then filled with salt. The next morning a weather forecast for each of the twelve months ahead can be made by observing the condition of the salt. The layers in which the salt is dry indicate fair months, while those with damp salt indicate rain. Anyone, of course, with grandmother's long experience in the kitchen knows what kind of an onion to select and which of the layers would have the most moisture, but it is still fun for the youngsters to wonder how grandmother does it.

Father has his little tricks also — such as tying bands of straw around the trunks of orchard trees to insure good crops during the coming year.

But the young girls have probably the most effective method of insuring their future happiness. By visiting nine different fountains, and taking three sips of water from each, while the church bells call the faithful to midnight Mass on Christmas Eve, a girl will find her future husband waiting for her at the church door. Since everyone in the village goes to midnight Mass, the young man who has been courting her need only to be standing at the church door at the right time to make everything turn out happily.

To give your tree a Swiss effect try some of the ornament ideas depicted on the following pages.

Snow-white birds
enhance the
Swiss tree.

27

Fill your home
with pure-white
Swiss splendor.

CANDY BASKET

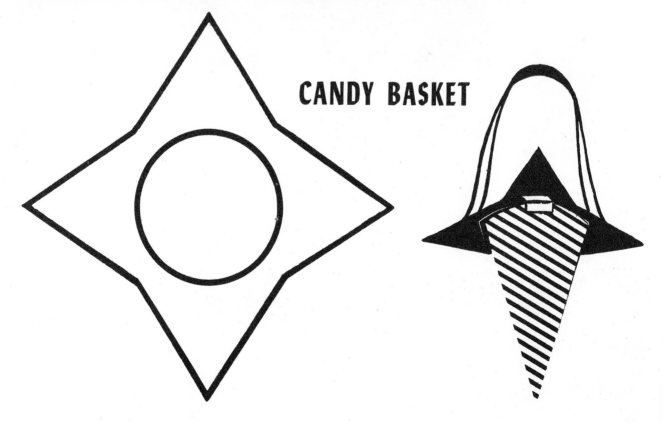

CANDY BASKET

Trace 4-pointed star for top. Make cone and tape to star. Suspend from tree branch with ribbon.

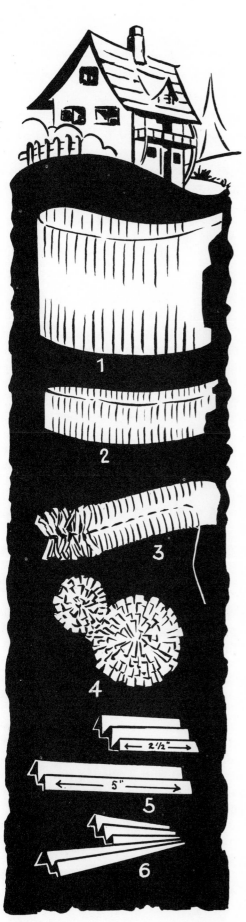

POMPON SNOWBIRDS

Body of Bird

1. Cut a strip of white crepe paper 3 in. wide by 24 in. long.

2. Slash paper on both sides. Gather up into a tight ball as in Figure 3 and twist a piece of spool wire tightly around the center. This forms the body of the bird.

Head

3. Cut a strip 1¼ by 12 in. and repeat *step 2* for the head of the bird.

4. Glue or wire small ball (head) to large ball (body). For the beak make a tiny cone.

Wings

5. For the wings cut two 2½ by 3-in. rectangles and two 5 by 2 in. Make ½-in. pleats and staple parts of wing together.

6. Use fine wire to attach wings to each side of the body.

Tail

7. Cut a 5-in. square and make ½-in. pleats. Gather at one end and wire to body.

ALPINE HAT

1. Design a simple border on a paper drinking cup using paint or crayons.

2. Fold point of cup down.

3. Staple a feather to folded tip.

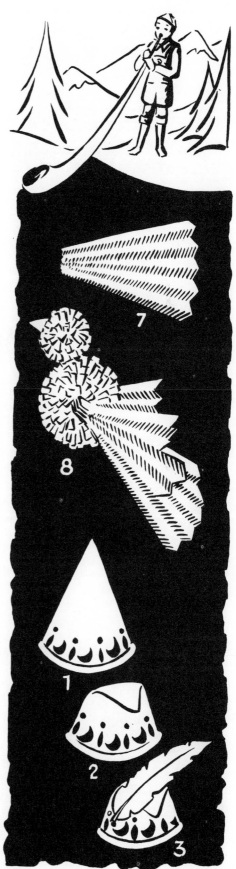

ITALY

"BUON NATALE"
or
"BONO NATALE"

THE Christmas customs of Italy are entirely centered around the Birth of the Infant Jesus. Even the Christmas greetings exchanged are an expression of this idea.

This concentration on the spiritual significance of Christmas in Italy is due to a number of factors, chief of which is the location of the papacy in Rome. The proximity of the Pope, as the visible head of the Church and his constant spiritual leadership in the early days of the Church, did much to stamp out the pagan customs, vestiges of which survived elsewhere.

To St. Francis of Assisi, also, should go much of the credit for this Italian emphasis on the real meaning of Christmas. It was his famous tableau in the little village church of Greccio in 1223 which originated our modern day crib scenes. St. Francis, in an attempt to bring alive the true meaning of Christmas to the people, constructed a crude but dramatic representation of the stable at Bethlehem in which live animals were used. The impact of this simple spectacle soon spread throughout the world.

As a result, Italy never did adopt the Christmas tree to any extent.

The weeks before Christmas itself are part of the spiritual preparation of the season of Advent. Shepherds come into the towns and villages to salute the shrine of the Virgin with bagpipes — after which similar musical visits are paid to the homes of carpenters in honor of St. Joseph.

A special novena, eight days of prayer and special church services, is held the eight days before Christmas ending on Christmas day itself. The children may go from house to house reciting Christmas poems for which they are rewarded with small coins. The twenty-four hours immediately preceding Christmas are observed with a strict fast after which a meal with many special dishes (but no meat) is eaten. This eve of Christmas is a family affair, and in former times there was always a kind of Yule log burning, known as the "Appo." The burning was observed with toasting in wine and wishes for the future.

Each Italian home has its "praesepio" or manger scene, as the center of interest, and there is considerable competition to see who has the best one. Figures for the praesepio are often hand-carved and include minute details in the features and dress of the Holy Family, the animals, and the shepherds.

Frequently, the manger scene, laid out in the shape of a triangle, furnishes the base of a pyramid-like structure known as the "Ceppo." This consists of a light wooden framework arranged to make a pyramid several feet high. Supported by this framework are several tiers of cardboard or thin slat shelves. The whole structure is decorated with colored paper, gilt pine cones, and miniature colored pennants. Small candles are fastened to the tapering sides. At the apex of the triangular sides is suspended a star or small doll. The shelves above the crib scene hold small gifts of candy, fruit, and presents.

This is in the old Tree of Light tradition which eventually became the Christmas tree in other countries. In many homes there is a Ceppo for each child in the family.

It is believed that the Ceppo came into existence as a substitute for the burning of the Yule log and that its pyramidal form represents the flames.

Another Italian Christmas tradition is the "Urn of Fate." This is a large

An Italian patchwork
of stars lights the
way for the newborn
King.

ornamental bowl in which wrapped presents for the family members are placed. Each then takes a turn in drawing until all the presents are distributed. In order to add a note of uncertainty to the proceedings, many presents are simply empty boxes, and with only one package permitted to be drawn at a time, the suspense of finding one's proper gift is a part of the fun.

The children, however, have still another gift-giving occasion to look forward to — the Feast of the Epiphany, January 6. On this commemoration of the Three Kings' visit to Bethlehem, the children hang up their stockings in anticipation of a kind of female Santa Claus, called Befana. She is depicted as a witchlike character riding around on a broom. The folk-tale origin of Befana is that the Three Wise Men on their way to Bethlehem stopped at Befana's hut to ask directions and, explaining their mission, invited her to accompany them. But the press of

household duties and the lateness of the hour prompted her to decline. A little later a shepherd also appeared and asked if she was not going to pay her respects to the Infant Jesus, and again she gave the no.

Finally, when it was dark, she saw a great light in the heavens and the clouds seemed to be a multitude of winged angels. She felt now that she had made a mistake in not going with the Wise Men, and, gathering up a few toys that had belonged to her own baby, who had died in infancy, she ran out to find the kings and the shepherd and join them in adoring the newborn King.

But Befana was unsuccessful in her search for the stable, and each year she returns on her never ending quest to find the Christ Child. So, as the children of Italy sleep, it is La Befana who comes in the night — still looking for the Infant — and it is she who leaves the gifts the children find in the morning.

STARS

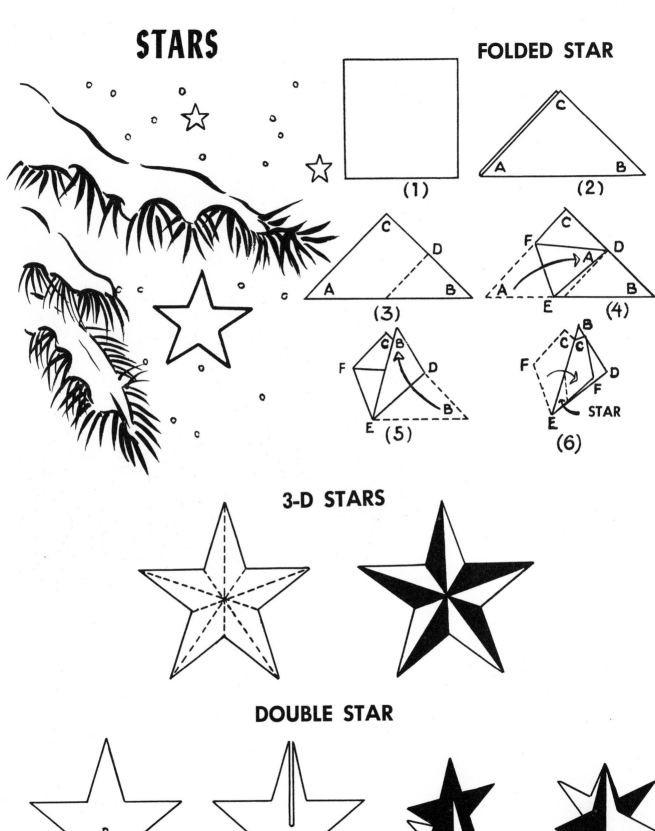

FOLDED STAR

(1)

(2)

(3)

(4)

(5)

(6) STAR

3-D STARS

DOUBLE STAR

1

2

3

4

32

SNOWFLAKES

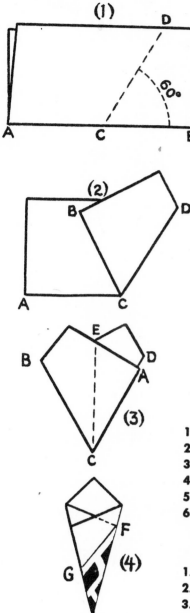

Lace from heaven.

FOLDED STAR

1. Use square of any size.
2. Fold diagonally.
3. Fold point *B* to point *C*. Mark crease *D*.
4. Fold point *A* to point *D*.
5. Lift point *B* and fold over.
6. Lift *FC* and fold over. Cut along dotted line for star.

3-D STARS

1. Draw a five-pointed star on white drawing paper.
2. With a dull metal instrument trace dotted lines from the center to each point.
3. Turn the star on reverse side and trace lines from center to crotches.
4. Crease long lines upward and short lines downward.

DOUBLE STARS

1. Make two stars from heavy paper. Cut slits as shown in Figures 1 and 2.
2. Insert one star into the other (Figs. 3 and 4).

SNOWFLAKES

1. Fold a 5-in. square of paper in half. Mark *C* — center of fold. Center protractor on *C* to mark 60-deg. angle. Place ruler on *C* and 60-deg. mark; draw line to edge of paper and mark point *D*.
2. Bring up corner *B* by folding on dotted line *CD*.
3. Lift point *A* to fold over *BC*. Fold in half on dotted line *CE*.
4. Cut on *GF*. Snip pieces out from folded edges. Open carefully.

33

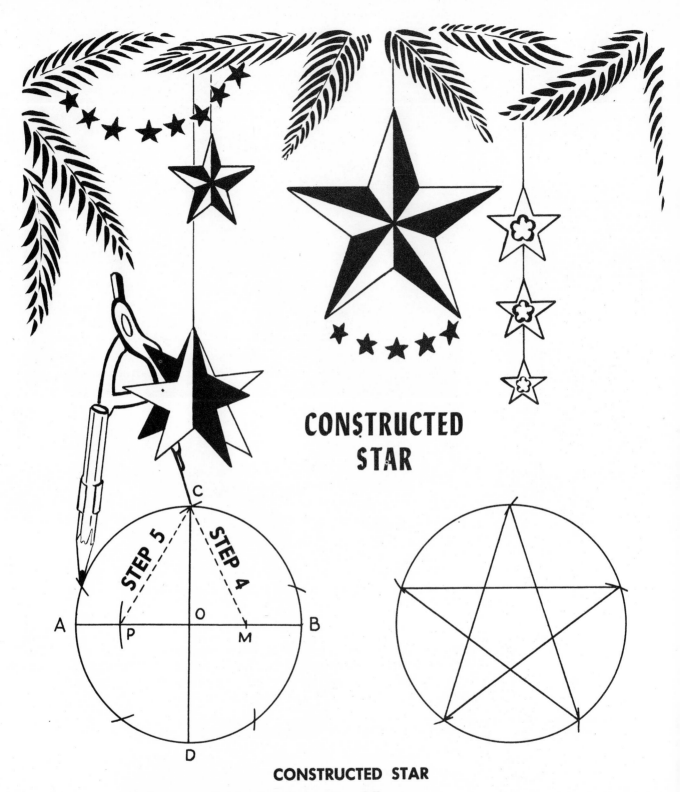

CONSTRUCTED STAR

CONSTRUCTED STAR

To construct a 5-pointed star proceed as follows:

1. Draw a circle of any size and label center *O*.
2. Draw diameter *AB* perpendicular to diameter *CD*.
3. Find the midpoint of *OB* and label it *M*.
4. Measure *CM* with a compass; place the point of the compass on *M* and draw an arc through *AO* and label the point through *AO* as *P*.
5. Measure *CP* with compass and use this length to divide circle into five equal parts.

CRÈCHE (PRAESEPIO)

IT WAS the absence of books and the illiteracy of the times which prompted St. Francis of Assisi in 1224 to dramatize the birthday of Jesus with the first manger scene. In his desire to bring home to the people of the little village of Greccio a realization of the humble beginnings of Christ and the significance of Christmas, he reconstructed the Bethlehem scene in a cave, using live animals and people to illustrate the Nativity.

The vividness of this experience, bringing the first Christmas to life, was so appealing that the idea spread throughout Italy, and then to Spain, France, Germany, and the entire Christian world.

At first those annual manger scenes continued to use live domestic animals and, as a result, began the legend that at Christmas time all animals joined in the worship of the Infant. They were said to receive the gift of speech at midnight on Christmas Eve.

Christmas cribs were first confined to churches and people brought gifts to the Infant Child, with the wealthy contributing jewels and robes for the costumes. Later hand-carved wooden figures came into use, many of them life size, and, as the popularity of the custom grew, there was great competition to produce the most elaborate and lavish manger scenes.

Many of the great castles of Europe had their own chapels, and to provide a suitable manger scene nobles and kings hired the leading artists of the times to produce lavish creations.

In this competitive spirit the artists of the seventeenth and eighteenth centuries rose to the challenge and the settings took a great variety of forms. Many figures were added to the Nativity scene, including representations of the nobleman who was financing the project, members of his household, and his servants. There were figures representing the various social classes, as well, all clad in the dress of the day, so that crib art became a kind of contemporary social history as well as a new art medium.

Movement was added to the figures by some ingenious craftsmen, and today some of the most famous examples of these Christmas cribs may be seen in museums throughout Europe.

One of the best known of these early cribs is now in Rome in the Basilica of Saints Cosmas and Damian. Forty-five feet long, twenty feet wide, and twenty-seven feet high, it includes several hundred figures, all hand carved of wood; its sky has stars and a moon; there are the traditional angels and shepherds; the surrounding countryside includes trees, farm animals, and people performing their daily tasks; there are buildings ranging from an inn to a castle, and a thousand other details.

Many families also made their own Christmas cribs and, in southern Italy particularly, the Christmas festivities centered around these home creations.

In Italy it is called the "Presepe" from the Latin *praesepio*, which means stable. In France it is the *crèche*; in Germany the *Krippe*; in Spain the *Nacimiento*. Wherever Christmas is celebrated today, there is a Christmas crib.

The Christmas crib was brought to America by the various immigrants who came to settle here. But there is one city in America which has become famous for its distinctive Christmas crib tradition — Bethlehem, Pennsylvania, appropriately named and now known as the Christmas City of America.

It was Christmas Eve, in 1741, that Nicholas Louis, the Count of Zingendorf, and a group of Moravian pioneers, seeking the religious freedom of the New World, named their settlement after the birthplace of Christ.

With them they brought their "Putz" tradition — the elaborate manger scenes carved of wood which have been handed down from generation to generation now, and which are still being improved as each family makes its contribution.

The most inspiring of these is the Community Putz which tells the Christmas story in seven scenes with more than two hundred buildings, the most noted of which is an accurately scaled reproduction of Herod's temple. A real stream of water runs through the Putz, which rests on fifty bushels of moss. It is annually displayed from December 16 to January 2 in the First Moravian Church there.

On the following pages we have presented some new ideas for making your own Christmas cribs. You can make them three-dimensional from a variety of materials or you may prefer to make a mobile, or modern, intriguing "stabile" to be used as a centerpiece on the table or mantle.

Whatever you choose as your artistic medium, it is a wonderful way to bring the true meaning of Christmas into your family circle and into your heart.

A reproduction of the Nativity scene in every home is
easily accomplished with small paper cones and Christmas balls.

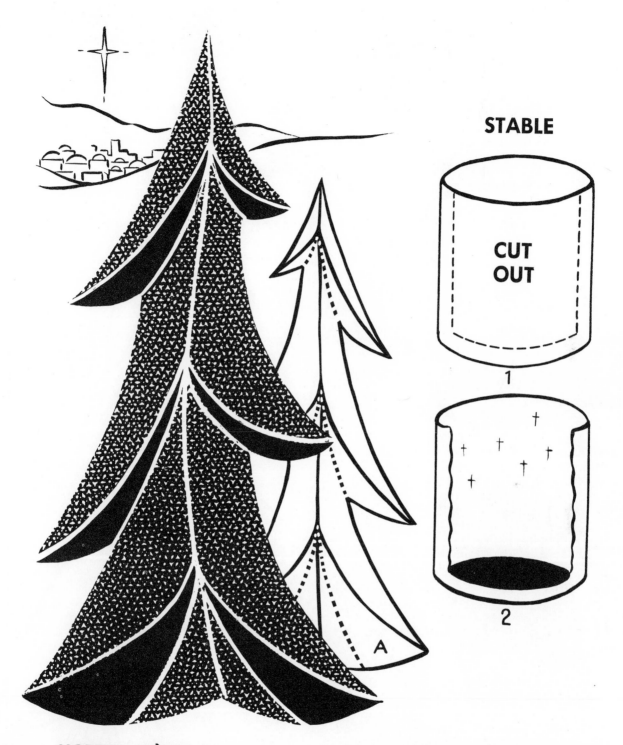

MODERN CRÈCHE (A)

Stable

Fashion a stable from an empty hat box or ice cream carton.

1. With a razor blade or sharp knife cut out one-third section of carton. Decorate sides with cotton.
2. Use blue construction paper for sky and dot with white stars.
3. For the roof and star support, make an arch measuring 4 in. in width from blue or white con-struction paper, and put it across open top of carton. (Length of strip depends on size of carton.)
4. Support arch with another paper strip in back of star (see photograph).

Trees

Cut out trees of various sizes and shapes. Score and fold up on solid lines; score and fold down on dotted lines (see diagram A). Group trees around crèche.

37

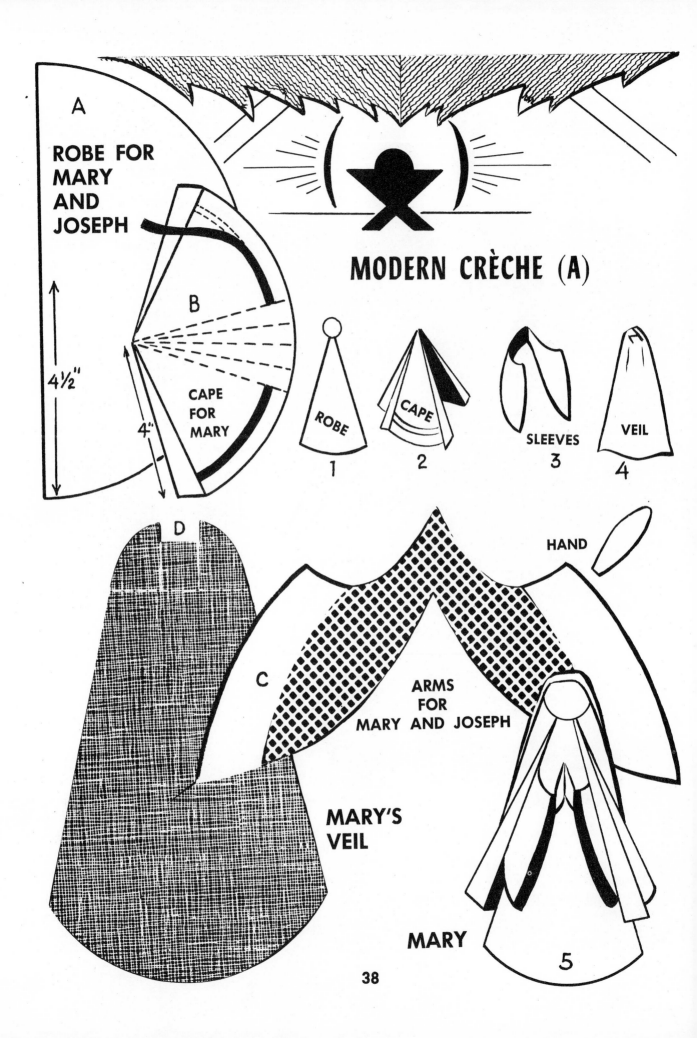

A
ROBE FOR MARY AND JOSEPH

4½"

4"

B
CAPE FOR MARY

MODERN CRÈCHE (A)

ROBE
1

CAPE
2

SLEEVES
3

VEIL
4

D

C
ARMS FOR MARY AND JOSEPH

MARY'S VEIL

HAND

MARY
5

38

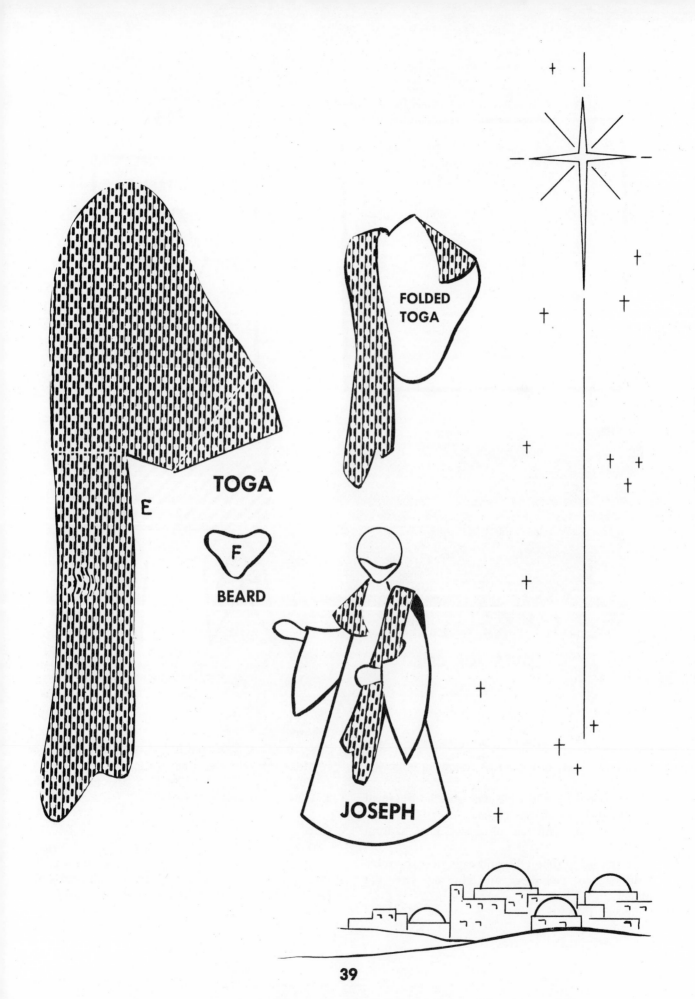

TOGA

E

F

BEARD

FOLDED
TOGA

JOSEPH

39

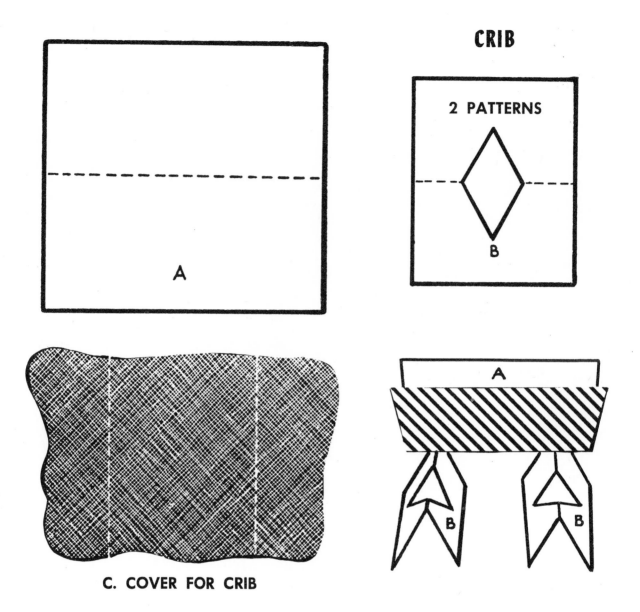

CRIB

2 PATTERNS

A

B

A

B   B

C. COVER FOR CRIB

Mary

Cut out *patterns A, B, C,* and *D,* following indicated
sizes.
1. Shape robe (A) into cone and glue head (small
   Christmas ball) on top of cone.
2. Score the cape and fold on dotted lines to form
   pleats.
3. Glue sleeves to robe (A), and cape over the robe.
4. Fold flaps of veil down and glue one over the
   other.
5. Glue veil to head.

Joseph

Cut *patterns A, C, E,* and *F,* following indicated sizes.
1. Make the robe and sleeves the same as Mary's.
2. Fold toga (E) on white lines and glue to robe.
3. Glue beard (F) to face.

Crib

Make one pattern of *A* and *C* and two patterns of
B. Fold on dotted lines. Assemble as shown. For
Infant, make a small tube and insert a Christmas ball
for head. Place Infant in crib and cover with *pattern C*.

SMALL CRÈCHE (B)

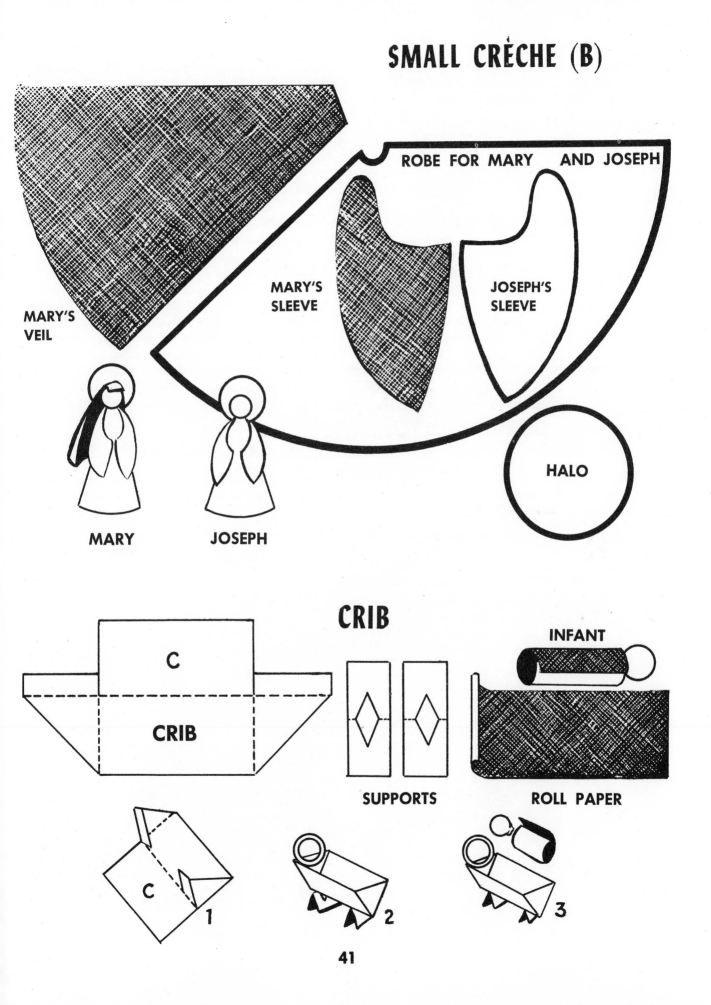

ROBE FOR MARY   AND JOSEPH

MARY'S SLEEVE

JOSEPH'S SLEEVE

MARY'S VEIL

HALO

MARY   JOSEPH

CRIB

C

CRIB

SUPPORTS

INFANT

ROLL PAPER

C   1

2

3

SPAIN

"FELICES PASCUAS"

THE "Noche-buena," or Good Night, is Christmas Eve in Spain. Following midnight Mass, the streets are alive with singing and dancing crowds celebrating the holiday, and around the crib or *nacimiento* in each home, the children sing Nativity songs to the music of tambourines and guitars.

Throughout the day and until the Twelfth Night the festivities continue as friends and relatives exchange the season's greetings.

A survival of Roman days is the Urn of Fate, similar to that customary in Italy. However, it is not gifts which are placed in the traditional bowl in Spain, but the names of friends and acquaintances. Two names are drawn at a time and the two people thus paired are expected to be especially friendly during the coming year. The right names may even lead to marriage if the one who draws the papers from the urn can be persuaded to do a little romantic cheating.

The favorite Christmas tradition for the youngsters, however, concerns the visit of the Magi to Bethlehem. Folk tales have it that each year the Three Wise Men repeat their journey and pass through Spain on their way. Hence, on the eve of the Epiphany, the children fill their shoes with straw for the camels of the Three Kings. The next morning the straw is gone and the shoes are filled with presents.

It was customary in some areas to dramatize the anticipated visit of the Three Kings. The children would march to the gates of the city carrying cakes for the kings, figs for the servants, and hay for the mounts. As the sun went down it was believed that they would see the kings silhouetted on some distant hilltop as they journeyed on their way to Bethlehem. Then as it grew dark, the children returned home, eating the sweets they had brought. Later they would go to church with their parents and sing "This morn I met the train of the Three Great Kings of the East" as they knelt before the manger scene, which now had the Wise Men added to the figures around the stable.

In many areas the children have a special fondness for Balthasar. He is shown riding a donkey, the familiar beast of burden in Spain, and it is he who leaves the presents for them in the night.

Spanish spangles
for pungent pines.

Singing spools
generate the
Christmas spirit.

Spain's age-long
tradition — Christmas
cribs and
tambourines.

CRIB SHRINE

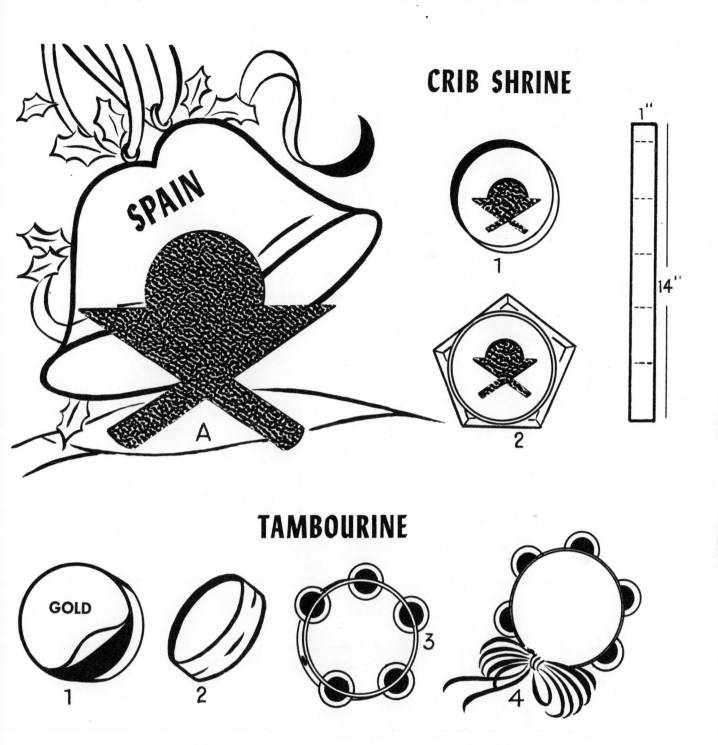

SPAIN

A

1"

14"

1

2

TAMBOURINE

GOLD

1

2

3

4

CRIB SHRINE

Cut a 1 by 14-in. strip of sturdy colored paper. Fold at 2½-in. intervals and tape around side of a round shallow box, thus forming a five-sided shrine. Trace crib A and glue to the center.

TAMBOURINE

1. For tambourine, use top of a powder box. Cover it with a gold circle.
2. Cut five evenly spaced slits on rim of box top, allowing space for a bow (Figs. 3 and 4).
3. Cut out five 1-in. circles from aluminum foil and ten ¾-in. circles from red paper. Glue a red circle to each side of the aluminum circle.
4. Place them in the slits and tie bow of narrow colored ribbon or yarn.

SPANISH GUITAR

1. Remove rim from small round cheese or powder box. Punch holes about ½-in. above center on each side of rim (see diagram).

2. Press both sides of rim slightly toward center. Insert a 3½-in. pipe cleaner through holes and bend each end of pipe cleaner back on rim. Figure now resembles a guitar.

3. Punch three evenly spaced holes at top and bottom of guitar. Make a slit about ¾ in. wide at top near punched holes. Use gold cord for guitar strings, as in Figure 4.

4. Add a bead to bottom and tie knot at end of cord.

5. Insert a popsicle stick through the slot slightly below pipe cleaner. Glue four beads to extreme end of stick. Glitter may be sprinkled on rim or other parts of guitar.

The fiddle strikes up a Yuletide welcome.

Magi — today.

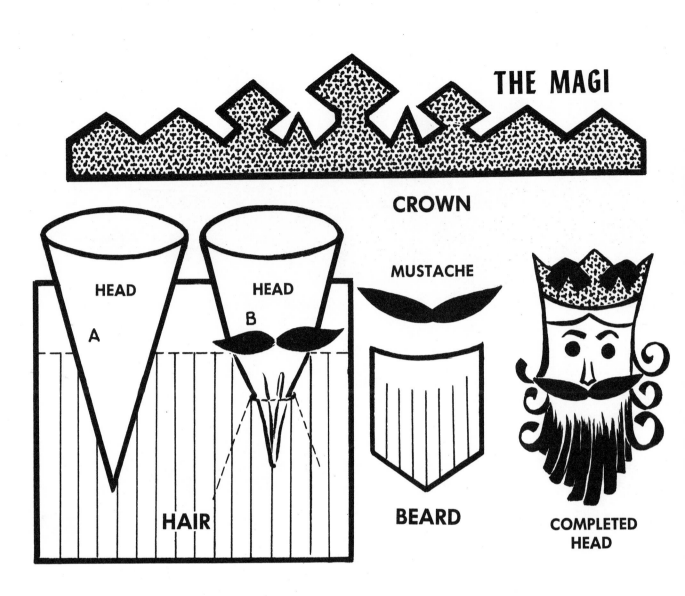

THE MAGI

To make bodies of the Magi, follow general directions given for crèche figures (see p. 40). Make bodies about 8 in. high.

1. *a*) From a fourth of a circle, having a radius of 3 in., make a cone for each Magi's head.
   b) Gather head cone at tip, and insert into body cone.
2. Trace crown, hair, mustache, and beard patterns. For hair and beard, fringe paper.
3. Paint eyes and nose on face. Glue beard, hair, mustache, and crown to head.

49

MEXICO

"FELIZ NAVIDAD"

CHRISTMAS festivities in Mexico begin on December 16 and every home is decorated with flowers, evergreens, and colored paper lanterns in preparation for the great day itself. A representation of the Nativity, called the *pesebra*, is also prepared in each household.

Thus begins the *posada*, which means resting place, and commemorates the journey of Mary and Joseph and their unsuccessful efforts to find a lodging for the night.

In some areas a group of villagers assemble and, carrying candles and chanting a song which asks for shelter, they go from door to door. But, of course, they are always told "there is no room." This *tradition* continues until Christmas Eve.

In many homes, the same ceremony is observed without leaving the house. Here part of the group of assembled friends and family members divide into two groups known as the Holy Pilgrims and the Hard-Hearted Innkeepers. Led by a white-clad figure representing an angel, the Pilgrims move through the house chanting, and the Innkeepers respond from a room designated as the inn.

After much coaxing on the part of the Pilgrims, who represent Joseph and Mary, the Innkeepers relent and the whole party kneels before the improvised altar with its *pesebra* and prayers.

Following this religious custom, a party is held with much singing, dancing, and games for the children. One of the features of this party is the traditional *piñata*. This is a large earthenware jar (*olla*) which has been fashioned especially for the occasion. It is disguised by means of paper and other decorative materials to look like a rooster, a bull, a clown's face, or whatever the maker may fancy. Inside the jar are nuts, fruit, and candy.

This is then suspended by a long rope from the ceiling and each child in turn is blindfolded, turned around a few times to confuse his sense of direction, and then given three chances to break the *piñata* with a stick. Since one end of the rope is controlled by an adult, there is considerable wild swinging to build up the excitement as the children flail away, but finally a lucky hit is made, the *piñata* shatters, and pandemonium results as everyone scrambles to pick up the goodies which have showered down.

As in Spain, the children receive their presents on the Epiphany.

Mexico's contribution to Christmas in America is a flower — the poinsettia. It is known in Mexico as the *Flor de la Noche Buena*, "the flower of the Holy Night," and there are several stories about its origin.

One is that a young girl, separated from her lover, died of a broken heart on Christmas Eve, and the blood drops which fell to the earth became the flower.

Another version is that as the people hurried to midnight Mass in the village church, carrying great armfuls of beautiful flowers to decorate the altars, they passed a small girl who inquired where they were going. On being told they were on their way to pay their respects to the Infant Jesus and that it was necessary to bring a gift of flowers, the little girl was heartbroken that she could not join them. But as her tears dropped to the earth, they were transformed into flowers of flame, which she gathered and brought to the Baby Jesus.

A gaily decorated Mexican tree.

The poinsettia was named after Dr. Joel Roberts Poinsett, the first American minister to Mexico, in 1825. Dr. Poinsett was intrigued with these "flame leaves" and sent cuttings to a nurseryman in Philadelphia, where it was named formally *Euphorbia poinsettia*, later botanically called *Poinsettia pulcherrima*. Credit for the propagation of the poinsettia in America is given to Albert Ecke, who raised the plant commercially on his farm near Los Angeles. This region in California is now known as the "poinsettia belt" and supplies the entire country with its plants. Several different varieties have been developed by the Ecke family and have been named after Albert and his wife, Henrietta.

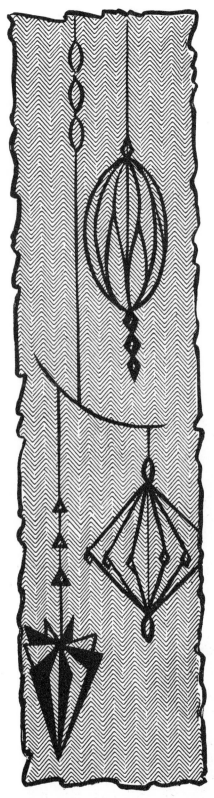

FESTIVE PIÑATAS

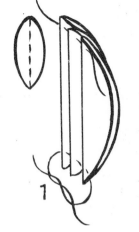 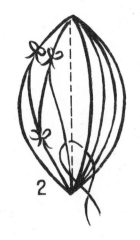 

FESTIVE PIÑATAS

1. Make twelve equal circles from colored construction paper. (Other shapes may be used.)
2. Fold each circle in half.
3. Thread all folded circles at top and bottom with heavy thread (No. 8 or No. 10).
   Tie snugly (see Fig. 1). Make yarn bows alternately.

MEXICAN SOMBRERO

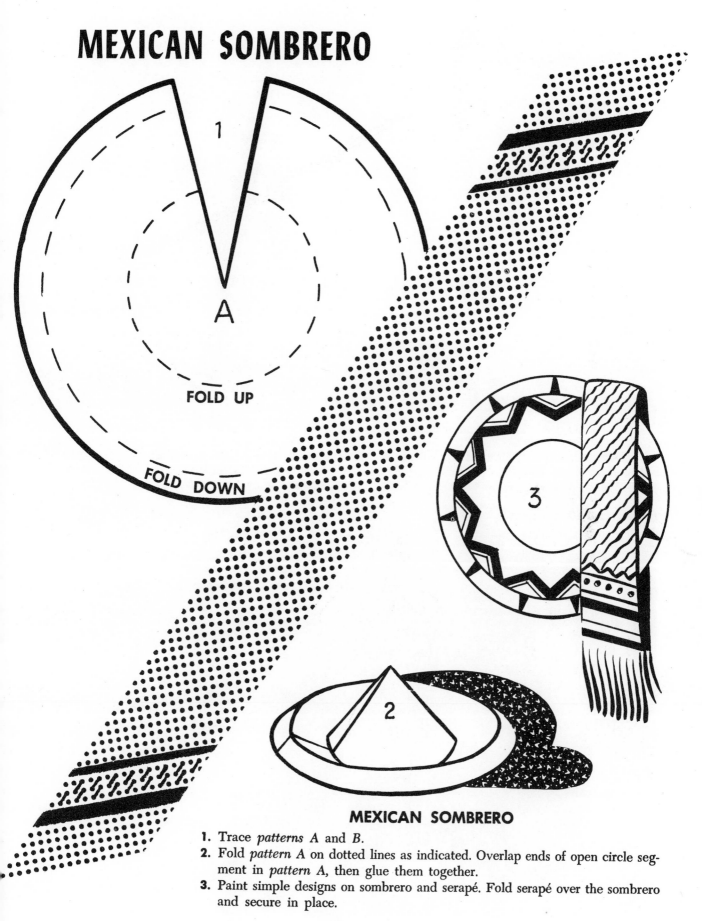

1

A

FOLD UP

FOLD DOWN

3

2

MEXICAN SOMBRERO

1. Trace *patterns* A and B.
2. Fold *pattern* A on dotted lines as indicated. Overlap ends of open circle segment in *pattern* A, then glue them together.
3. Paint simple designs on sombrero and serapé. Fold serapé over the sombrero and secure in place.

Sombrero window piece.

Gifts wrapped Mexican style.

54

"JOYEUX NOËL"

FRENCH Christmas traditions are a blend of those of her northern and southern neighbors and a few from the east, in addition to those of her own. This may be due to her location, or perhaps to the nature of her people and the merging of artistry and emotion which has made France famous.

The celebration of Christmas begins with midnight Mass on Christmas Eve, followed by a traditional supper known as *Reveillon*. Special foods served at this meal include oysters, sausages, and wine. In many places, however, this comparatively simple repast has been replaced by the baked ham, roast fowl, salads, fruit, bonbons, and pastries usually associated with the Christmas day dinner. Sidewalk cafés and restaurants in the city remain open all night for those who prefer their *Reveillon* in the gay atmosphere of the streets. It is interesting to note that the name given to this meal stems from a word which means "to wake up" which in the military life is "reveille" — the first call of the day. The *Reveillon* supper of French Christmas tradition is also a symbol of spiritual awakening to the meaning of Christ's birth.

Even the poor had their *Reveillon*. It was customary to parade a large wicker figure of Melchior (one of the three kings) from door to door. Melchior was strapped to the back of a donkey along with food hampers which were filled at the various homes he passed. This food was then distributed at the church to those in need.

The Yule-log tradition was also observed, particularly in the rural areas. The entire family went out together to select the tree, which was then cut down by the father and the oldest son. Arriving home, it was carried in with much ceremony by the male members ranged by age along its length. The room was circled three times and then the log would be put in the fireplace, where a glass of wine was poured over it as the family sang a Christmas song.

Different provinces had variations in their Yule-log tradition. If there was a girl of marriageable age in the family, she might sit on the log while a toast to her prospects was drunk by the family and friends.

Sometimes, after the log was blazing well it was pulled out to permit the children to beat it with sticks — the resulting sparks symbolizing the departure of evil spirits, a residue of heathen rites.

Its heat was used to prepare the *Reveillon* and even the ashes had value, for when sprinkled at the base of fruit trees, they insured a fruitful yield in the coming season. Yule-log charcoal was also saved as a home remedy for certain ailments, especially those associated with chilling, and were good for humans and animals alike.

Although the Yule-log tradition was well observed in the French country areas, the scarcity of such fuel and the disappearance of fireplaces in city homes gave it a new interpretation.

Here special cakes, shaped like logs, were baked and then covered with chocolate icing to look like bark and in this way the Yule log became a favorite Christmas delicacy, possibly furnishing the inspiration for that well-known pastry of today — the chocolate eclair.

In the old days French children received their gifts from Le Père Noël, "Father Christmas," who was accompanied by Le Père Fouettard, or "Father Spanker," whose function it was to reward the bad children. The gifts were small tokens, toys and goodies left in the children's wooden shoes. In more recent times, it is the Christ Child, "Petit Noël," or "Le Petit Jesus," who leaves these gifts for French children.

Artistic avalanche from France.

Adult gift-giving occurs on New Year's day, which is another dinner occasion, and the season then moves on to the Fête des Rois. This Festival of the Kings, known also as Twelfth Night, is marked by the most elaborate dinner of the season, one which most prefer to partake in a restaurant.

It is customary at this meal to have a special cake in which a bean is hidden. The cake is cut into as many pieces as there are persons present at the table. Whoever finds the bean becomes the king or queen of the Twelfth Night festivities, chooses a partner, and then everyone must carry out the wishes of the reigning monarchs for the occasion.

The Christmas tree was not too well known in France until comparatively recent times because evergreen trees were not readily available and were too expensive for importation. Styles of tree ornamentation were also imported.

An artistically appealing French motif can be made by using only imitation snowballs or white bonbon ornaments, with much tinsel added for sparkle.

Another idea presented here is to use the French coat of arms of the former royal family, the "fleur-de-lis," which can be given a very colorful treatment in metallic papers and varying sizes.

These ideas serve to give a French flavor to a Christmas tree but have no historical significance as ornaments, other than their association with La Belle France, which in a sense is reason enough.

56

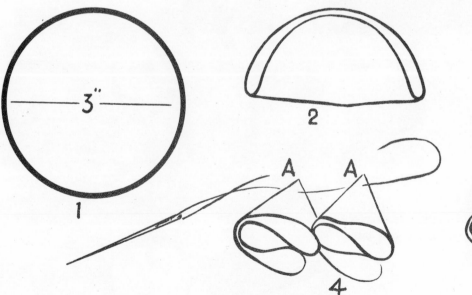

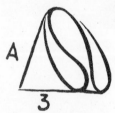

CELLOPHANE BALLS

1. Make twelve circles 3 in. in diameter.
2. Fold circles in half without creasing them.
3. Then fold in quarters.
4. String the 12 folded circles at point A.
5. Form them into a ball.

Dancing dolls made of
transparent plastic
and pipe cleaners.

A ballerina centerpiece
will grace your table.

FRENCH BALLERINA

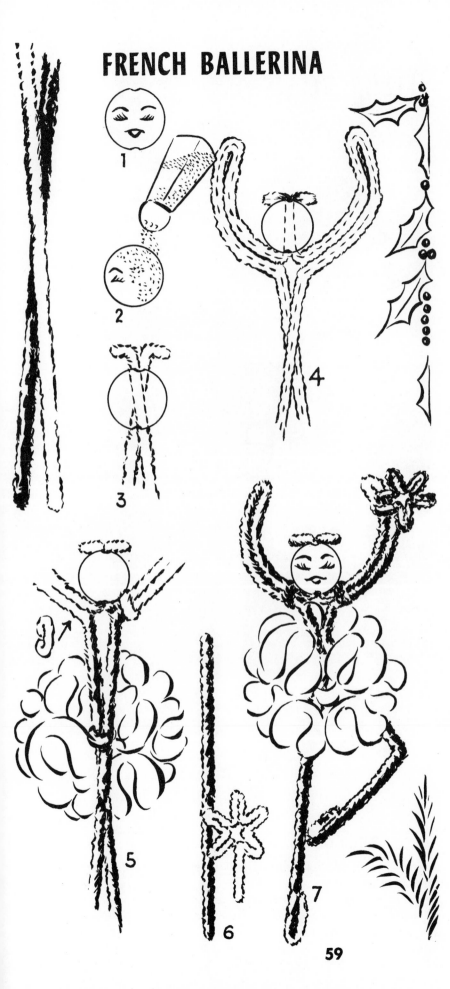

FRENCH BALLERINA

1. Paint eyes, eyebrows, and mouth on a wooden bead.
2. Cover back of head with glue. While still moist, sprinkle with glitter.
3. Bend tips of two 12-in. pipe cleaners to form right angles. Slide pipe cleaners through head. Anchor bead at these right angles.
4. Following dotted lines in Figure 4, shape arms of ballerina.
5. Make small pipe cleaner clamps to hold arms in place.
6. Form a small poinsettia from a 4-in. pipe cleaner and fasten to hand of doll.
7. Place a drop of glue in the center of the cellophane ball to hold body together. Shape legs.

FLEUR-DE-LIS

FLEUR-DE-LIS

1. Cut three (A) patterns — red, gold, and blue. Glue wings of *pattern* A together to form a three-sided ornament.
2. For treetop, enlarge pattern to desired size. Crease red pattern in center and mount on large gold pattern, thus giving a three-dimensional effect. Glue paper rosettes, sequins, or other decorations down center of treetop pattern.

ST. NICHOLAS came to Belgium from Germany and has managed to retain the robes, the pastoral staff, and miter of his episcopal rank.

Actually the children expect St. Nicholas to make two appearances. The first, two nights before December 6, constitutes an examination visit to separate the sheep from the goats, in a sense — that is, to determine who are the good and bad children.

Then, on the eve of his feast day, the children place their shoes, baskets, or dishes in hopes that the good bishop will fill them from his never empty sack. To make sure they won't be passed by, water, hay, and carrots are placed outside the door to attract the attention of St. Nicholas' gray horse or white donkey. This sounds like good psychology — even from children.

If the following morning finds the room in disorder, with chairs tipped over, it shows that St. Nicholas has been there. The good children find candy and small toys in their shoes or baskets, while, theoretically, the bad ones will find switches.

Christmas day itself is a religious holiday marked by children's processions to the churches. The children are colorfully dressed and march in groups, each holding a ribbon streamer attached to a central figure such as a shrine, crucifix, or image of a saint. One boy is selected to personify St. John the Baptist and he carries a crucifix and leads a white lamb. The chimes of the Cathedral in Antwerp sound ninety-nine bells to mark the beginning Christmas services.

St. Nicholas is represented on the Belgian Christmas tree in a variety of ways — the traditional gingerbread man of Germanic origin, and with paper and other materials as the white-bearded, red-dressed figure of the mythical Germanic "Thor."

Interesting items found on the Belgian tree are the ornaments shaped like horns, bells, and drums. Although these are typical New Year's eve aids in America, their origins go back to pagan days when such devices were used to frighten away evil spirits during the winter solstice rites. Stars, nuts, and clowns also symbolize the gaiety of the Christmas season.

Flemish — "VROLIJKE KERSTMIS"
French — "JOYEUX NOËL"

Musically adorned Belgian tree.

"Ring out the bells."

BELLS

1. Trace circle on gold paper. Make circular snips toward center.
2. On an 18-in. red ribbon, string beads, cupcake liner, and gold circle over cup to form attractive bell.

62

BELGIUM

DRUM

ACCORDION

6"

2½"

1

2

3

DRUM

1. Paint top, bottom, and side of powder box. Glue narrow colored strip around entire side of box. With needle and heavy thread stitch alternately top and bottom of box (Fig. 1).
2. Use ¾-in. ribbon for strap. Hold in place on both sides of drum with round stickers.

ACCORDION

1. Cut a strip of colored construction paper 6 by 2½ in. Score ½-in. spaces for pleating.
2. Cut out two narrow strips and glue on rectangular piece ½ in. from each side (Fig. 1).
3. Pleat accordion and glue a paper band to each side for handles.

JOLLY SANTA

SANTA MOBILE

1. Trace and cut one large star and four small ones. For small stars see directions for 3-D stars (see p. 32).
2. Cut out eyes, nose mustache, and mouth; arrange on face. Glue face to point of star (see Fig. 3).
3. Use fringed paper for fur and beard. Attach belt and buckle across center of star.
4. Cross two 5-in. pipe cleaners and tie at point of crossing. Suspend Santa from center and 3-D stars from four points of pipe cleaners.

"ZALIG KERSTFEEST"

SINT NIKLASS AVOND is, of course, the eve of St. Nicholas in Holland, and is family party night for the children in anticipation of a visit from the good Saint, as well as for the older people who have their fun, too.

Holland has preserved the episcopal robes of the saint and he generally arrives on his white horse, sometimes with a cartful of presents (previously ordered). Since he arrives early in the evening in many places, he will be followed by a crowd of happy, noisy children.

In some parts of Holland, however, he may arrive by boat, having made the long journey in that fashion from Spain, and in this case he will be attended by his Moorish servant, nicknamed "Black Pete," whose function is to punish the bad children.

As in Belgium, the children leave hay and carrots in their wooden shoes for St. Nicholas' horse. In return they expect candy and small toys or possibly a lump of coal, although, strangely enough, there is no record of anyone ever actually having found coal, an indication probably that there are no bad children in Holland — at least during this season.

When the children are tucked away for the night, St. Nicholas may drop in with "surprise" packages for the older generation. In this visit, however, he does not use the chimney for his traditional entrance but thumps the door knocker and then discreetly disappears.

The packages are then brought in and distributed, one at a time, in order to enjoy the full flavor of watching the recipient open it and wonder from whom it was sent. The spirit of the occasion is to make these packages as mysterious as possible and the giver frequently disguises his identity through rhymes and riddles. A favorite trick is to make up a package of many boxes, each carefully wrapped, sometimes in several layers of wrapping, with a different name on each layer so that the suspense can build up as the person named unwraps and then passes it to the next one named.

Tea and special varieties of hard cookies are served during the "unwrapping" period of this gift-giving. The table is then loaded with delicacies of the season, such as "letterbanket," small cakes made in the form of initials, hot chocolate, and roasted, buttered, and salted chestnuts.

Other cookies of this season are flat hard cakes known as "Klaasjes," originally formed in the image of St. Nicholas on his white horse, but now made also in various bird, fish, and animal forms.

Christmas itself is observed strictly as a religious holiday and is marked by the traditional family dinner and social visiting.

Marzipan, the famous Yuletide almond-paste delicacy known in many European countries, as well as in America, is a Dutch favorite. Once such confections were used in wooing; the young man sent an image of a Dutch boy to his prospective sweetheart and if accepted she returned him a similar girl image.

DUTCH DUET

An array of delightful Dutch ornaments.

DUTCH DUET

Trace patterns of Dutch boy and girl on heavy colored paper. Paint features. Hang in pairs on tree.

HOLLAND

WINDMILL

1

2

PIN WHEEL

1

2

3

4

A tree worthy of a Dutchman's praise.

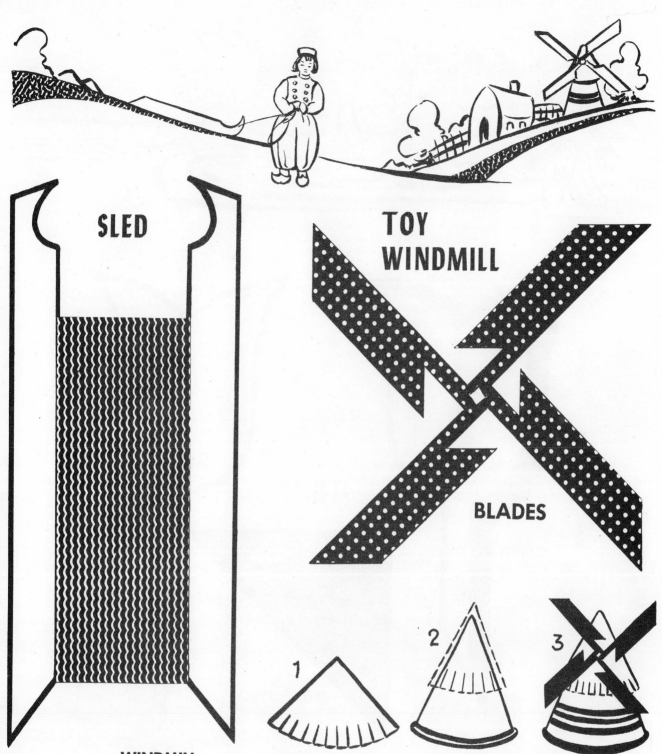

SLED

TOY WINDMILL

BLADES

1

2

3

WINDMILL

Trace and cut Figures 1 and 2. Attach Figure 2 to Figure 1 at *x*. In Figure 2, curl ends slightly.

PIN WHEEL

Trace Figure 1 and cut on diagonal lines as indicated. Bring one corner at a time over the center and glue corners together (Figs. 2 and 3). Attach bead to a piece of fine wire and pierce through ornament for hanging (Fig. 4).

TOY WINDMILL

1. From a semicircle make a cone half the size of a paper drinking cup. Fringe edges, as in Figure 1.
2. Paste fringed cone over cup (Fig. 2).
3. Attach blades to fringed cone with shanks or rivets. (Construction paper may be used for cone and blades.)

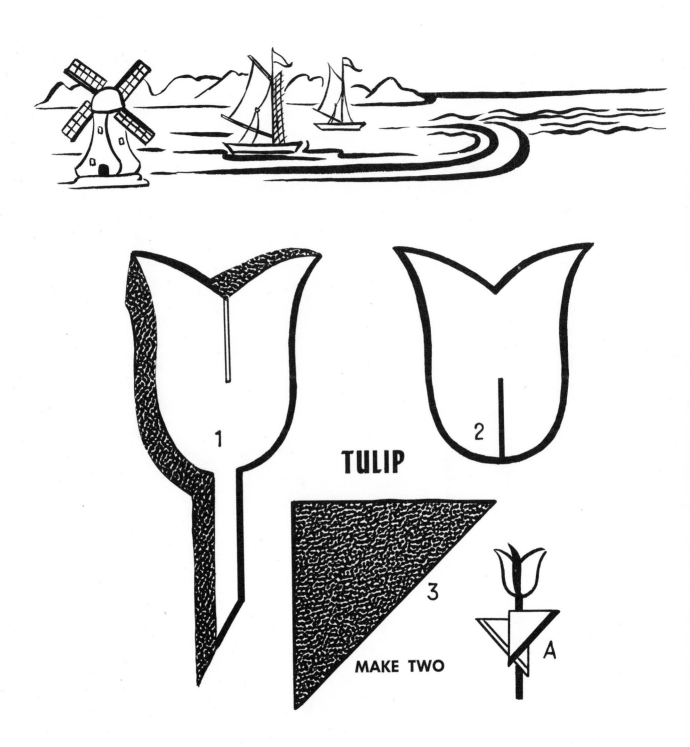

TULIPS

Trace Figures 1, 2, and 3 (two of 3). Cut out and slide Figure 2 into Figure 1. Glue leaves (Fig. 3) to stems and arrange as in Figure A.

"MERRY CHRISTMAS"

THE Christmas tree came to England from Germany in 1841 when Prince Albert of Saxe-Coburg set up a tree in Windsor Castle for Queen Victoria. It was immediately popular and, while its decorations were at first those of the Prince's homeland, it wasn't long before it acquired a distinctive tradition of English origin — that of using Christmas cards, many of them bearing pictures of the royal family, as its ornaments.

The first Christmas card is credited to England although there is a considerable disagreement as to the individual who should be recognized as its originator. Even the exact date is disputed, but the first card appeared between 1841 and 1845. According to the *London Times* which once attempted to settle the problem, credit should be given to John Calcott Horsely of the Royal Academy who was commissioned to produce a card for Sir Henry Cole, in order that Sir Henry might save himself the chore of writing a personal letter to each of his many friends.

It was a German immigrant who made Christmas cards popular in the United States. Louis Prang opened a small lithographing shop in Roxbury, Massachusetts, in 1874. He successfully worked out a process of making colored pictures for his cards and produced a series of simple floral designs which became immediately popular. Within a few years he was printing five million cards a year and had made Christmas card production his major operation.

The use of Christmas cards for tree decoration has also become popular in America. Small trees, decorated with cards, are now being provided by thoughtful people to hospitals and similar institutions to bring some of the Christmas spirit to those who must remain shut in during the holidays.

England is also noted for the food traditions it has brought to Christmas.

Henry VIII introduced the boar's head served with an apple in its mouth to the dinner menu. It was brought to the festive board in ceremonial style while minstrels and choristers joined in the presentation. The special significance attached to the boar, considered to be the most ferocious of animals, dates back to pre-Christian history when it was offered to the goddess Freya at the winter solstice.

Another ancient Christmas food of early English royalty was the peacock which was roasted whole and then redecked in its brilliant plumage. It was customary for the knights to take the "vow of the peacock" — by making their pledge of the year with their right hand on the peacock. Thus began the custom of making New Year's resolutions.

Roast beef is now the traditional English Christmas meat and it was another English monarch who gave the name to one of the most succulent roasts. This was Charles II who, in a humorous mood, surrounded by his admirers at Christmas dinner, compared his affection for them to his fondness for a loin of good beef. With his sword he touched the huge roast before him and parodying the ritual of knighting, proclaimed: "I knight thee Sir Loin." Thus we have our sirloin steaks today.

Another favored English dish for Christmas was the plum pudding which originally began as a dish called "frumenty" consisting of boiled wheat, which was strained and combined with milk and egg yolks. Gradually new ingredients were added to spice it up but it was not until 1670 that it became the culinary achievement known in recent times.

CONTINUED ON PAGE 74.

ENGLAND

ENGLAND'S MINIATURE TREES

1. Trace and cut four patterns of tree. Fold each in half.
2. Glue together to form a three-dimensional tree.

3-D FLAKES

Trace and cut *pattern A* and *pattern B*. Insert small circle into large one in place marked by dotted line, then suspend the completed ornament.

English tree topped with a fairy.

ENGLAND'S
MINIATURE TREES

1

2

3-D
FLAKES

A

B

73

CONTINUED FROM PAGE 71.

The story of the origin of plum pudding has often been told. An early English king, hunting the day before Christmas, became lost in a blizzard and was unable to return to his castle. One of the members of his party, acting as cook, attempted to make the best of the meager provisions he had by throwing everything into the pot and cooking it together. This involved the remains of a stag, previously killed, flour, apples, dried plums, eggs, ale, brandy, and sugar. Tying the mess in a bag, he boiled it into a pudding and thus was acquired another Christmas recipe. So, at least, runs the story!

Mince pies were first known as mutton pies and were thought of as edible symbols of the gifts of the Wise Men in that their spices represented the choicest products of the East. They were first baked to represent the manger, with crossed lines on the upper crust symbolizing the hayrack of the stable.

The "wassail bowl" is another item of old English tradition, but actually it originated with the early Norsemen when the Princess Rowena, presenting a bowl of hot spiced wine to Prince Vortigern, saluted him with the expression "Wass-heil," which was a toast to his well-being. The prince responded with "Drinc-heile" in saluting her. Completely charmed by her beauty, he married the girl. So, today, we have the wassail bowl at our parties and potable toasts to the health of all present.

Although carol singing had its origin in several European countries in early times, it achieved a special popularity in the rural areas of England. Strolling groups of carolers, known as the "waits," moved through the village streets singing, and many of the carols still popular today were thus preserved.

Still another old English custom is that of presenting mystery plays at Christmas. These were given by actors known as "Mummers" because they were masked. As a rule they portrayed St. George slaying the dragon, or in pantomime they acted out the death of Nature by Winter and its subsequent renewal of life by Spring.

Such plays, and the masquerade costumes of the Mummers, have their origin in the Roman pagan celebration of the Saturnalia. The masquerade balls we still have in our country, and particularly the Mardi Gras celebrations, serve as a reminder that even our fun making has its roots deep in history.

* * * *

In Scotland, the first person to enter the home on Christmas morning shouts "First Footing" and presents a gift for the household to insure its future happiness. Those who leave the house during the day and return must remember to bring something in with them also, even though it is only a stick of wood for the fire, or some food.

The personality of the "first footer" had a variety of implications. The most desired one was a man, preferably with black hair. If he was robust and cheerful, it was especially propitious. In return for the luck he brought into the house he was given a good, stiff drink which had to be downed in one swallow. Obviously a good first footer in making his rounds absorbed a considerable amount of Christmas cheer, so that the custom generated its own spirit of conviviality.

Scotch needles and plaids.

IRELAND

"NODLAIG NAIT CUGAT"
or
"BEANNACT OE' ORT"

IRELAND is one of the few countries that never adopted the Christmas tree as a national tradition.

As in Italy and Spain, the celebration of Christmas in Ireland is essentially a commemoration of the birth of Christ, and the manger scene is the one center of interest in Irish homes.

But Ireland has contributed a popular custom to our American Christmas, that of placing a light in the window on Christmas Eve.

This custom originated when the English in their attempts to suppress the religious beliefs of the Irish, forced the priests to conceal their identities. In secret, and at night, priests would visit the farmhouses and homes of Ireland to conduct religious services.

Thus at Christmas time, the Irish family, hoping that Mass might be said under their roof, would place a lighted candle in the window as a guide and a sign of welcome for any priest in the neighborhood.

When the English soldiers inquired about the candles, they were told that should Mary and Joseph come that way looking for shelter, the candle was an invitation to enter and be welcomed. Thus, the custom was permitted as merely "Irish superstition." Later, when religious toleration again came to Ireland, the custom remained and was brought to America by Irish immigrants.

Another Irish custom is known as "feeding the wren." This is based on a legend about St. Stephen, whose death as Christianity's first martyr is commemorated on December 26. The story goes that St. Stephen attempted to hide from his enemies in a bush, but was betrayed by a chattering wren. To help the wren do penance for this treason, it was customary for Irish children to take a wren in a cage from home to home, collecting money for charity.

Since Ireland has no Christmas tree of its own, we thought it would be interesting to design one, based on symbols which have become associated with Ireland. Hence the shamrock, clay pipes, and leprechaun faces, topped by the Irish country hats. They're all easy to make and in green and white colors will give you a tree with the spirit of the Emerald Isle.

A truly Irish spectacle with garlands of
green and white shamrocks.

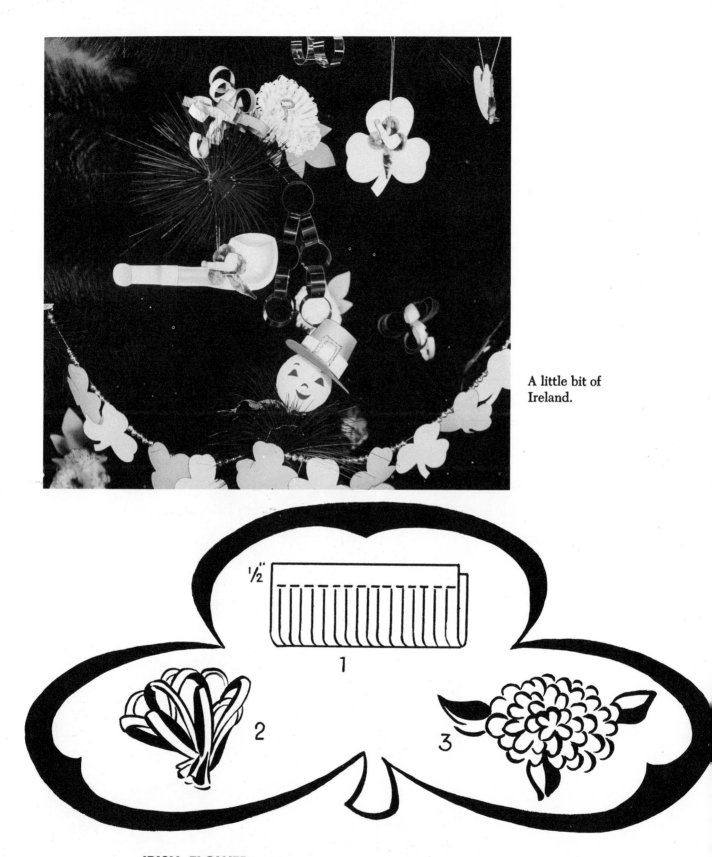

A little bit of
Ireland.

IRISH FLOWER

1. Use tissue paper or wide ribbon 4 by 4 in. and fold in half. On folded side cut ¼-in. strips, stopping within ½ in. of open edge.

2. Gather open end to form a cluster and bind with fine wire.

3. Arrange seven clusters together to complete flower. Green leaves may be added.

HOLIDAY SHAMROCK

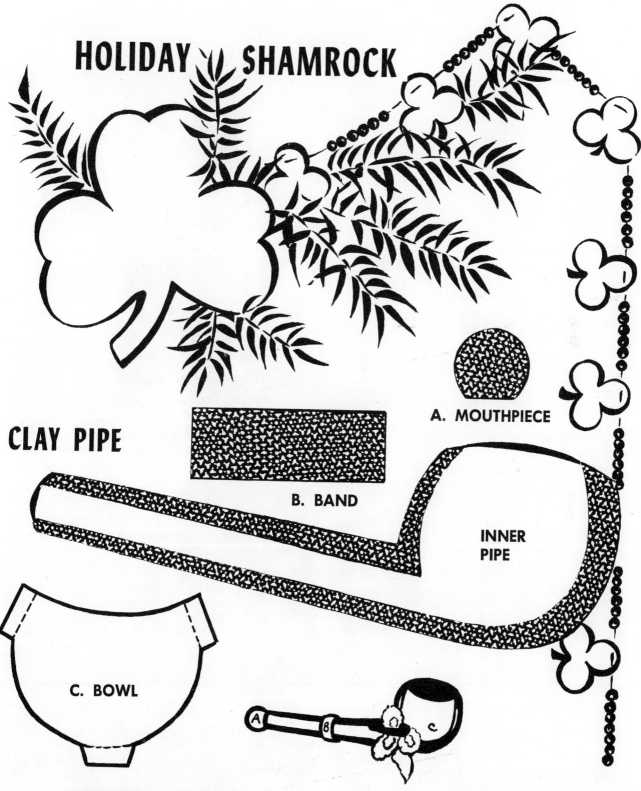

CLAY PIPE

A. MOUTHPIECE

B. BAND

INNER PIPE

C. BOWL

HOLIDAY SHAMROCK

Adorn your tree with striking green and white shamrock chains. Trace large shamrock and string between green or gold beads.

CLAY PIPE

Trace patterns of pipe, mouthpiece, band, and bowl. Turn tabs of bowl under and glue to inner pipe. Glue band (B) around pipe stem. Attach mouthpiece to tip of stem. Add shamrocks or other typically Irish trimmings.

Home decorations

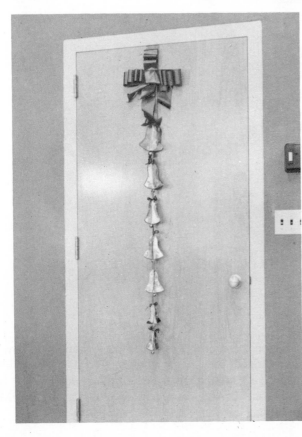

THE customs, like the languages of the various Scandinavian countries, are very similar.

The days before Christmas are spent in hectic preparation of traditional foods: sausage, cheese, bread, cookies, and special dishes for the huge dinner to be served on Christmas day.

In Norway, for example, there is "flat bröd," a thin bread made from oat flour and baked over a slow peat fire. Huge quantities are made at Christmas time to be available the year round. There is also "lefse," made of mashed potatoes, salt, cream, and flour, rolled pie-crust thin and baked like a waffle, and served with syrup and sausage at the Christmas breakfast. Rice pudding with lingen berries is a favorite dessert, accompanied by a multitude of Christmas cookies.

Christmas dinner in Sweden begins with the famous smörgåsbord which during the holidays becomes a feast in itself. There is an elaborate assortment of cheeses, anchovies, herring, and other spiced fish and caviar. Next is lutfisk, which is dried cod served with a milk gravy. The meat course is roast pig or goose and sometimes both. And the traditional drink is Julglogg, popularly abbreviated to "glogg," which is made from brandy and port wine, a variety of eight or more spices, and almonds and raisins. Finally there is the famous Swedish coffee, cleared with egg white, and accompanied by cookies.

Special thought is given to the birds and animals at Christmas time. The farm animals get extra rations and, as in many European agricultural areas, there is a tradition that on Christmas Eve at midnight, the animals may speak so as to add their voices to all those giving homage to the Infant King.

For the birds there is a bundle of grain tied to a long pole and set up in the farm yard so that they, too, may feast, safe from the clutches of cats who may not have absorbed the full spirit of peace on earth.

Christmas trees have long been traditional in the Scandinavian countries where evergreens grow abundantly. Miniature flags are a part of the decorations.

On the tip of the Norwegian tree it is customary to place three candles, representing the Three Wise Men. Other decorations may include little elflike creatures dressed in red, with pointed caps and long white whiskers. These are the *Jule-nissen* — the invisible, troublemaking mischief lovers who make strange thumping noises in the attic, overturn the milk, sour the cream, and account for the countless minor mishaps common in a home with small children. The Jule-nissen ride about on Jule-buken, or goats, and bad children are likely to get bumped by these creatures.

Favorite tree ornaments as well as table decorations in Sweden include the *Jul-docka,* straw dolls in many forms — boys, girls, chickens, goats, and other animals.

*   *   *   *

In Sweden the Christmas season really begins with St. Lucy's day, December 13, when the eldest girl in each home dresses in white, with a red sash, and dons an evergreen crown with nine candles. It is her duty on Christmas morning to wake the family and bring them coffee and cakes. Many communities choose a Lucia Queen for the pageant and parade held in St. Lucy's honor. St. Lucy was an early Christian martyr who refused to give up her religion to marry a pagan, and was burned at the stake by the Emperor Diocletian.

Lucy's story was brought to Scandinavia by the missionaries and had such a strong appeal to the Vikings that she became the patron saint of all maidens. Because her feast day came on a day previously observing pagan rites to the goddess of light (about the time when the daylight hours begin to increase) the tradition of wearing the crown of candles became a part of the Lucia custom.

Norwegian —
"GLEDELIG JUL"

Swedish —
"GLAD JUL"

81

"'Twas the night before Christmas."

ANTLER

PATTERN OF REINDEER

Little Mr. and Mrs. Norway.

SPIRIT OF NORWAY

YARN DOLL

1. For body, wind yarn 30 times on 6-in. cardboard.
2. Remove cardboard and tie neck.
3. For arms, wind yarn 15 times around 4-in. cardboard.
4. Remove from cardboard and tie at both ends (Fig. 4).
5. Insert arms.
6. Tie waist. Clip loops to form skirt.
7. For legs, separate yarn and tie ½ in. from bottom.
8. Embroider eyes, nose, and mouth with colored thread.
9. Dress dolls with scraps of brightly colored material.

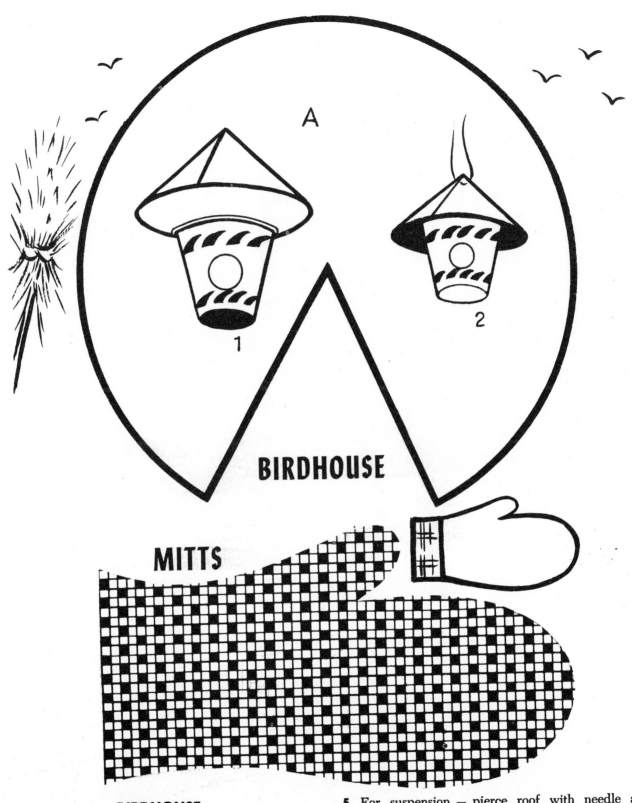

BIRDHOUSE

1. For roof, trace *pattern* A from construction paper. Shape into shallow cone and glue ends together.
2. Attach roof to top of small paper drinking cup.
3. Paste a colored circle to side of cup.
4. Paint border design along top and bottom of cup.

5. For suspension — pierce roof with needle and thread. Tie ends of thread together.

MITTS

Trace pattern of mitten. Decorate with wallpaper or paint a design. Suspend in pairs on tree.

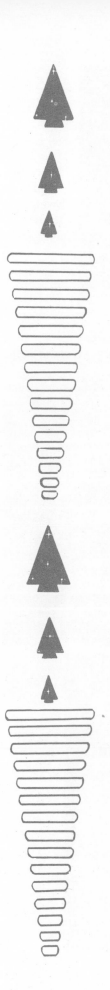

Sweden decked with the natural beauty
and delicacy of straw.

Elegantly
simple
Swedish
straw
designs.

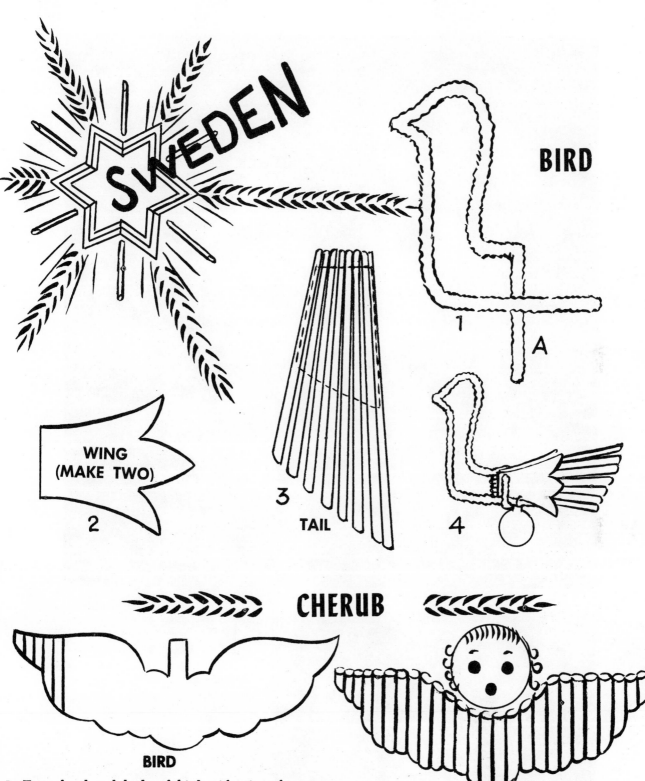

SWEDEN

BIRD

WING (MAKE TWO)
2

TAIL
3

1
A

4

CHERUB

BIRD

BIRD

1. Form head and body of bird with pipe cleaner (see Fig. 1).
2. Trace two patterns of wings.
3. On one side of a small cardboard base (dotted line in Fig. 3), glue straw into a fan shape and trim.
4. Glue tail between wings. Then fasten wing-tail unit to pipe-cleaner body by bending section A of pipe cleaner around wings. Suspend a Christmas ball below wings on extended pipe cleaner (Fig. 4).

CHERUB

Trace pattern of wings on heavy paper. Measure straw to fit wings vertically. Fasten with glue. (Both sides of pattern may be covered with straw.) Attach a wooden bead for the head.

Sweden's straw
characters.

ROOSTER

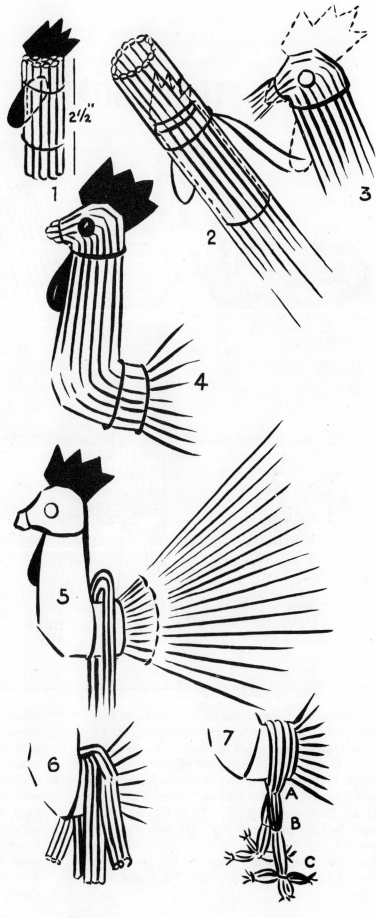

1. **Neck Form.** Tie a bundle of straw to form a cylinder about ¾ in. in diameter and 2½ in. long. Make combs from heavy red paper and insert into top of straw bundle (Fig. 1).

2. **Neck.** Encircle cylinder with one layer of straw 14 in. in length. Bind with red ribbon or cord (Figs. 2 and 3).

3. **Head.** Bend straw down to form head. Tie firmly.
   Beak. Snip off excess straw to form beak.
   Eyes. Glue red circle on each side of head for eyes (Fig. 3).

4. **Body.** To form body, see Figure 4.

5. **Tail.** Tie straw securely in sections (Fig. 5). Trim to desired shape.
   Legs. Take three 8-in. pieces of wire and bend in half over body as shown in Figure 5.

6. Take six 3½-in. straws and slip one over each wire. Cover wired straw with three additional straws that measure 8½ in. in length (Fig. 6).

7. Fasten each leg at *points A, B,* and *C.* To form foot, divide straw into three parts at *point C.*

91

STRAW GOAT

GOAT

1. **Goat Pattern.** Enlarge and cut pattern 12 in. long and 10 in. high from heavy cardboard (Fig. 1). Glue crushed newspaper to both sides of cardboard to give three-dimensional effect.
2. **Neck.** Form neck by encircling the cardboard with two layers of very long straw. Fasten with wire.
3. **Head.** Bend ascending straw (*A* in Fig. 2) downward to form head and nose. Tie nose and trim straw.

   Body. Bend descending straw (*B* in Fig. 2) over body form to cover newspaper. Tie firmly with wire.

4. **Hind Legs.** After covering body, bend straw downward and separate it into two parts to form hind legs. Tie each leg securely. Cut off excess straw.
5. **Forelegs.** Pierce front part of body with heavy wire, 20 in. in length. Bend wire downward to form legs. Insert wire through straw bundles which measure 10 in. in length (Fig. 5).
6. **Horns and Tail.** To form goat's horns, make a straw braid 30 in. long. Fasten to head as in Figure 6. Make smaller braid for tail (see photograph).
7. Cover all wired areas with red ribbon.

DENMARK

"GLAEDELIG JUL"

DENMARK'S Christmas traditions closely resemble those of Sweden and Norway because of their common ancestry. One contribution of Denmark to America, however, has accomplished an immeasurable amount of good work throughout the world.

That is the Christmas seal which is sold each year for tuberculosis work in more than forty countries, and is used by millions of people to carry on the fight against what was once considered a hopeless disease.

The idea originated with Einar Holboell, a postal clerk, in 1903. The following year the first Christmas seals, bearing the portrait of Queen Louise in a wreath of roses, were for sale in the post office of Denmark. More than four million stamps were sold the first year, raising about $18,000 for tuberculosis sufferers. Sweden adopted the idea that same year, to be followed, two years later, by Norway.

It was a Danish immigrant to the United States, Jacob Riis, an editor and social worker, who introduced the idea in America. He wrote an article entitled "The Christmas Stamp" describing the work the seals were doing in Denmark and suggesting that the idea be tried here.

The first American seal, with a half wreath and a cross, was designed by Emily Bissell, of Wilmington, Delaware, whose personal enthusiasm was responsible for its introduction on December 7, 1907, at the Wilmington post office. She was successful in interesting the Red Cross in supporting Christmas seal sales in co-operation with the newly organized National Tuberculosis Association. Since 1920 the Tuberculosis Association has conducted the sale alone and relies on this annual campaign for its chief support.

Today some three thousand groups are affiliated with the National Tuberculosis Association and the disease has dropped from first to seventh place as a cause of death in America.

From the family workshop —
these and many more.

MERRY MOBILE

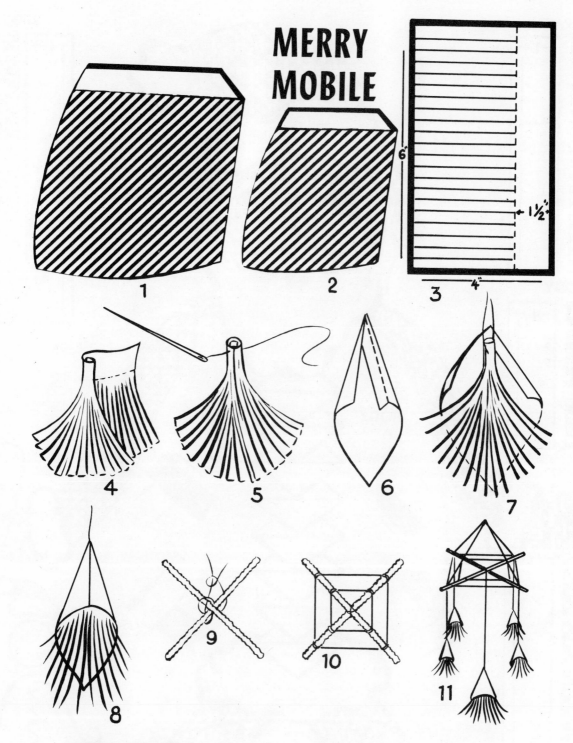

MERRY MOBILE

1–3. Trace *pattern 1* once and *pattern 2* four times. Enlarge pattern 3 to 4 by 6 in. and fringe edges. Make five.

4. Roll fringed pieces into tassels.

5. Thread tops of tassels and tie.

6. Shape *patterns 1* and *2* into cones. Fold on dotted lines.

7. Insert tassels into cones.

8. Fasten cone around tassel.

9. To make a support for mobile, cross two 4-in. pipe cleaners, then tie center securely with fine wire.

10. To insure balance, fasten threads or wire around pipe cleaner as in Figure 10.

11. Suspend small bells from ends of pipe cleaners and large one from center. String mobile from four ends of pipe cleaners. Tie all strings together 3 in. from point of attachment.

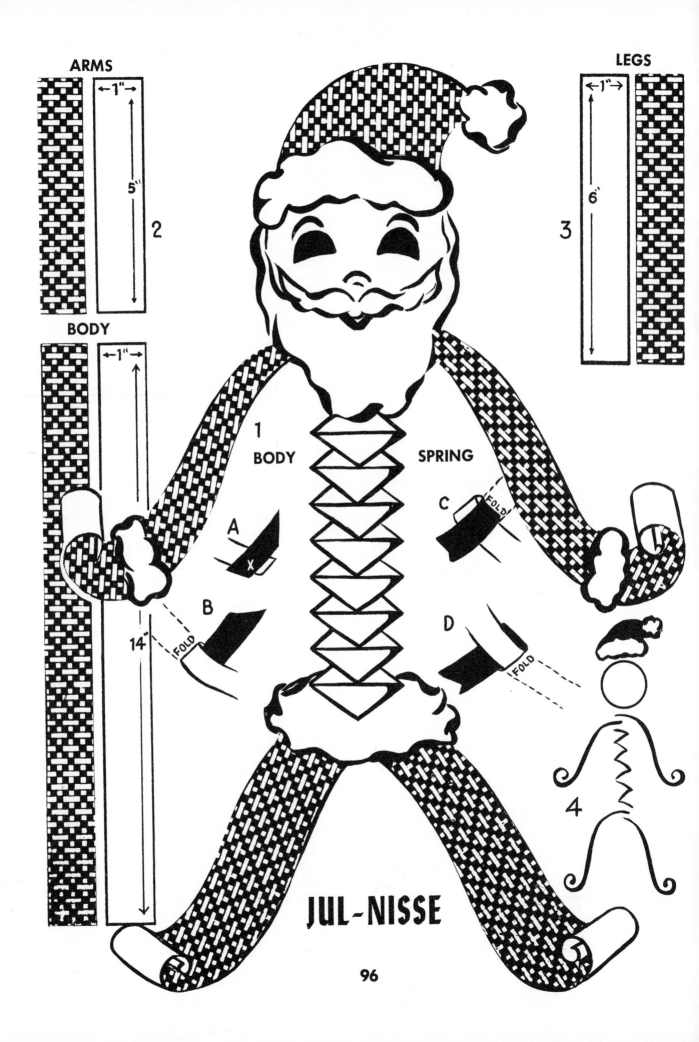

ARMS

← 1" →

5"

2

LEGS

← 1" →

6'

3

BODY

← 1" →

1

BODY   SPRING

A

B

FOLD

14'

C   FOLD

D

FOLD

4

JUL-NISSE

96

DANISH BASKETS

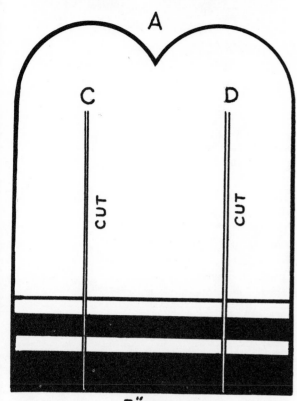

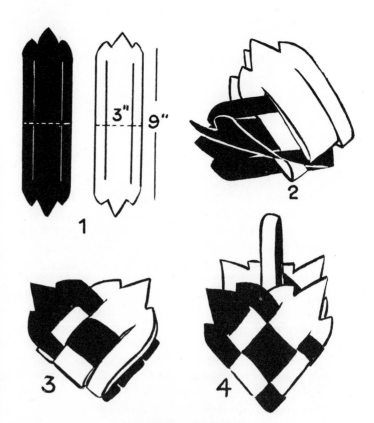

DANISH BASKETS

1. Cut two pieces of paper 9 in. long and 3 in. wide. (Vary design by using two colors.) Fold papers in half and trace *patterns* A or B keeping folded edge on the bottom. Cut three or more 3-in. strips (see D and C in Fig. A).

2. Take both patterns, one in each hand, and weave strips together by slipping the first light strip through the first dark strip. Open the light strip and slip the second dark one through it. Then hold the light strip together again and slip it through the third dark strip (Fig. 2).

3. Take the second light strip and reverse the above method (Fig. 3).

4. Take the third light strip and repeat step 2. To make handle, cut a 6 by ¾-in. strip and fold in half. Glue folded strip to basket (Fig. 4).

JUL-NISSE

1. For body spring, cut two strips of paper 1 in. wide and 14 in. long. Paste together at *point X* to form a right angle. Fold light strip over dark one, then dark over light. Continue folding to desired length.

2. Make a hat and jolly face.

3. For arms, cut two paper strips 1 in. wide by 5 in. long. For legs, cut two strips 1 in. wide by 6 in. long.

4. Attach arms to top of body spring and legs to lower part. Attach head. Decorate figure with cotton as shown in diagram.

FINLAND

"HAUSKAA JOULUA"

CHRISTMAS in Finland begins with a bath. First the house is thoroughly cleaned, even washed. Then, as a part of the Christmas Eve preparations, the entire family takes a Finnish bath, known as the *sauna*. Perhaps steaming is a better description, for the traditional Finnish bathhouse is a separate building with three rooms. In one room are placed stones that have been heated until red-hot, and then water is poured over them to fill the room with steam. The next room is for rubbing, and the bather uses a small switch of birch twigs to strike the body and increase circulation. Before entering the third room for dressing the bather takes a roll in the snow for further stimulation.

Once everyone has enjoyed this traditional *sauna,* a light meal of barley porridge and almonds, with cream and sugar, fish, and prune tarts, ends the fasting. It is said that during this meal it is possible to see visions — the person one will marry during the coming year, or, if one looks out the window, someone who will die during the coming year. But this gift is reserved only for a few, and they must fast the whole day before, which may account for these apparitions.

Suspended from the ceiling over the dining table is a light wooden framework, covered with straw to symbolize the stable where Christ was born. Paper stars are hung from this fixture, and these, reflecting the light of the lamps and fire below, give a suggestion of the night sky as the family eats its simple meal.

Following supper, there used to be wrestling matches by the men on a straw-covered floor, on which the children would later sleep in imitation of the Christ Child. The women would blacken their faces and, dressed in men's clothes, visit their neighbors. No words were spoken on this occasion, nor would they accept any food. This odd custom was a commemoration of the Moorish Wise Man.

On Christmas day, the church services were held at dawn. Horse-drawn sleighs would carry the family groups to church making a wonderful sound as they sped over the crisp snow. It was customary to attach as many bells as possible to the sleigh for this occasion and the countryside itself seems to jingle merrily as the faithful gathered for the service. Each house on the way blazed with light from the candles placed in every window.

Following church, the sleighs raced home for the Christmas meal of ham or roast suckling pig with Lingenberry relish and other favorite foods. Dessert was a rice pudding with a single almond, and the one who found this in his portion could expect good luck during the coming year.

It is "Father Christmas" who generally brings the children their presents, but in some parts of Finland he is known as *Wainamoinen* from Kalevala folklore, or again as *Ukko*. He is represented as an old man with a long white mustache, a white peaked cap with blue trim, and a red coat. The legend of Wainamoinen is believed to have served as the prototype which Longfellow immortalized in his poem of Hiawatha.

Finland's traditional
"Father Christmas" and
the tree.

FINLAND'S FANCIES

TAIL

TAIL

TAIL

SANTA

BASKETS OF BEAUTY

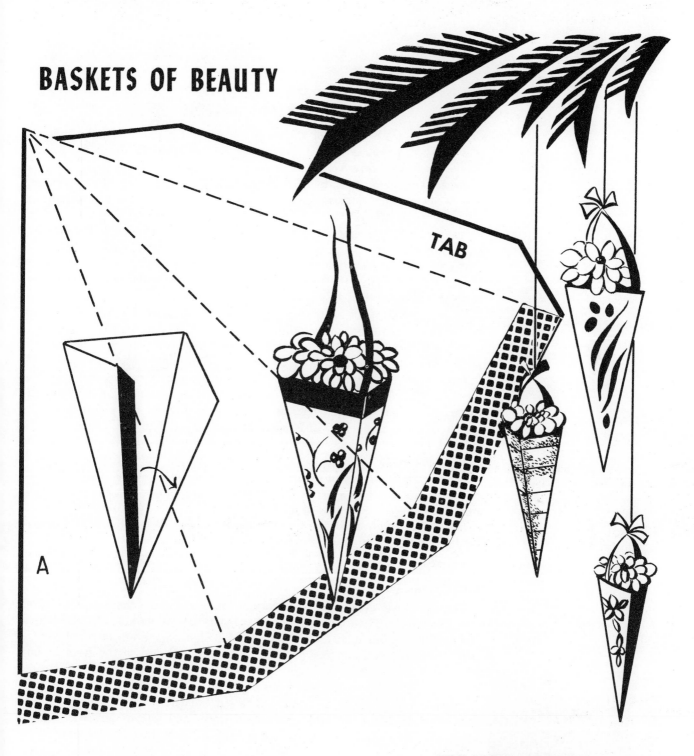

TAB

A

BASKETS OF BEAUTY

1. Trace and cut pattern from any colored paper. Fold on dotted lines. Glue tab to opposite edge (A).
2. Paint or sponge simple designs on all three sides. Fasten pompon. (Flower directions for top of cone are found in section on Ireland.)

FINLAND'S FANCIES

BIRD

Trace patterns and fold on dotted lines. Turn wings back and head down. Glue tail to wings.

SANTA

Trace cap and face. (Use white drawing paper for face, red for cap.) Paint features. Use pipe cleaners for beard and mustache. Secure them with glue.

101

LITHUANIA

"LINKSMŲ KALĖDŲ"

CHRISTMAS EVE is one of the most important Lithuanian family holidays. It is a day of peace, good will, preparation, and intimate family spirit.

The *kūčia*, or Christmas Eve dinner, is the highlight of the day. The table is spread with sweet, fresh hay (as a reminder of Christ's manger), and covered with a snow-white cloth reserved for the occasion. A crucifix and a plate of holy wafers (*plotkelės*) are placed in the center of the table. *Kūčia* is commenced after the evening star has appeared in the sky. The head of the family begins the meal with a prayer of thanksgiving for all the blessings of the past year and adds a wish that the family remain intact during the ensuing year. He breaks and shares the wafers with each member of the family, and they, in turn, with each other.

The menu consists of twelve courses (symbolizing the twelve Apostles): soup, fish, vegetables, *šližikai* or *preskučiai* (small hard biscuits served with poppy-seed and honey sauce), *kisielius* (oatmeal pudding), etc. The meal is leisurely, with conversation flowing in an atmosphere of absolute peace and good will.

Because of the mystic aspect of the evening, old traditions, superstitions, legends, etc., are revived. Straws are drawn from under the tablecloth; the length of the straw determines the length of life; or, to the young folk — the length of their single life. Girls carry kindling wood into the house to count; an even number of sticks indicates marriage during the coming year. Children run frequently to the well to taste the water to see whether it had changed into wine; or to the stable to eavesdrop on the animals. At one mystic moment on Christmas Eve, the water was believed to change into wine and the animals would converse in the tongue of man.

The entire family made every effort to attend the *Piemenėlių Mišios* (Shepherd's Mass) at midnight or at dawn.

Christmas day was spent at home or visiting neighbors; before admittance to a home, visitors were required to sing a Christmas carol. Gifts were distributed only to children.

The Christmas ornaments of Lithuania are perhaps the most unusual of all tree decorations. These are made of wheat or rye straw, gathered by the women and artistically fashioned into hundreds of designs. Some are made of various lengths of straw strung together with needle and thread in the form of bird cages, bell towers, stars, and other geometric shapes. Fanciful birds are created with eggshell bodies and wings from paper or feather fluffs.

Another way of using the straws is to cut them into very small pieces and glue them on end to a paper pattern of traditional folk design, such as the tulip. The ends then are slit and bent back to make tiny starlike units.

Still another treatment is to glue lengths of the straw together to make three-dimensional pieces. These may be simple crosses or elaborate projects reproducing the wayside shrines found on Lithuanian country roads. Even figures can be built up of various straw lengths in this way.

The artistic effect of the green Christmas tree, entirely decorated with such straw ornaments, is very effective. Soda fountain straws make an ideal substitute for wheat straw and are not as fragile. A light coat of shellac or varnish applied to such soda straw ornaments adds to their durability.

Another way of adapting these Lithuanian ornament ideas is to use colored plastic straws. With the tree lights shining through these a very unusual effect can be obtained.

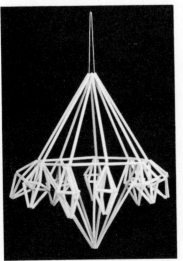

The Lithuanian tree of airy straw mobiles.

Preparations for a geometrical creation.

Make a perky bird by:

1. Puncturing each end of an egg,

2. Blowing out the egg content,

3. Making two more holes for the wings,

4. And inserting feathers for the head, tail, and wings.

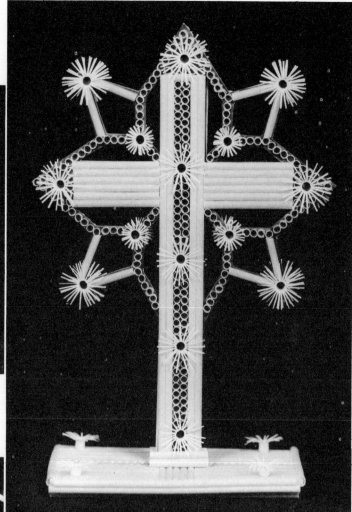

Rays of shooting glory accentuate the Lithuanian wayside shrine.

A miracle in straw — Lithuanian lacy daintiness.

From straw to the beauty, charm, and grace of a demure dancing doll.

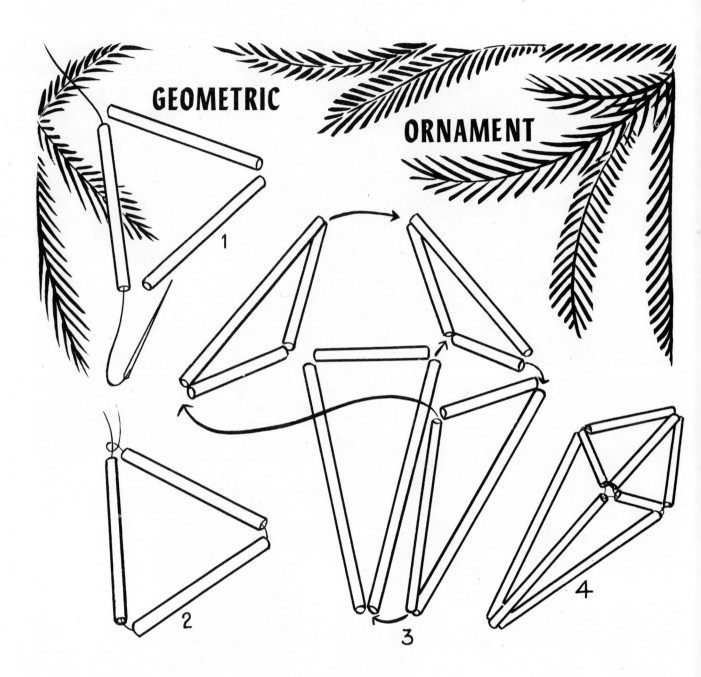

GEOMETRIC ORNAMENT

Use eight short drinking straw segments of equal length and four long segments of equal length.

1. String three short straws to form an equilateral triangle.
2. Make another triangle exactly like the first.
3. Take the two remaining short pieces and the four long ones. String two long straw segments and one short segment to form an acute triangle. String two more long straws and one short one to form another acute triangle. Connect the four units as in Figure 3.
4. Tuck strings inside straws.

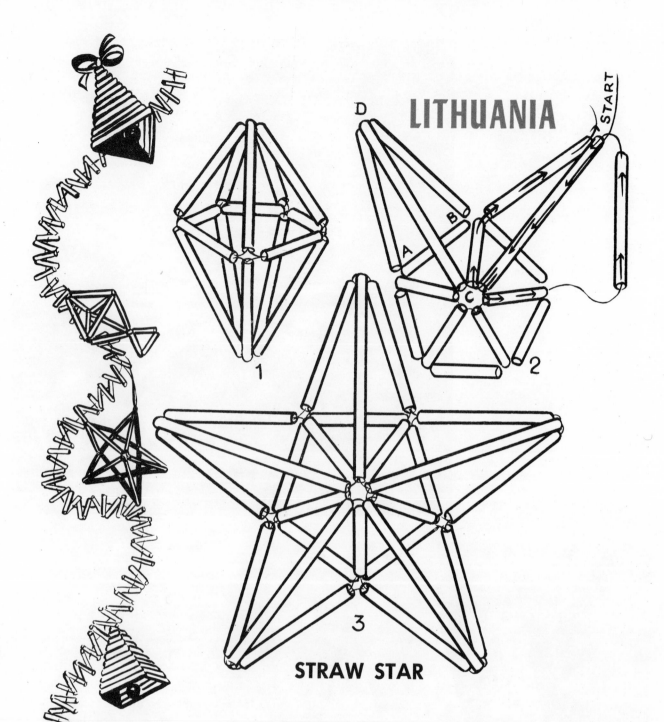

LITHUANIA

D

START

A B C

1

2

3

STRAW STAR

STRAW STAR

1. Use drinking straws to make a small five-sided ornament (Fig. 1). Add one side to the geometric ornament just described.
2. Measure two equal straw lengths to extend from *points A* and *B* to *point D* (see Fig. 2). Measure two longer straws to reach from *point C* to *point D*. Follow arrows in Figure 2 for attaching straws. Turn star on reverse side and attach remaining long straw.
3. Repeat step 2 four more times until all five points are completed.

"What delicate beauty!
You'd be cautious too."

Elegantly simple is
the styrofoam array.

WONDER TREES

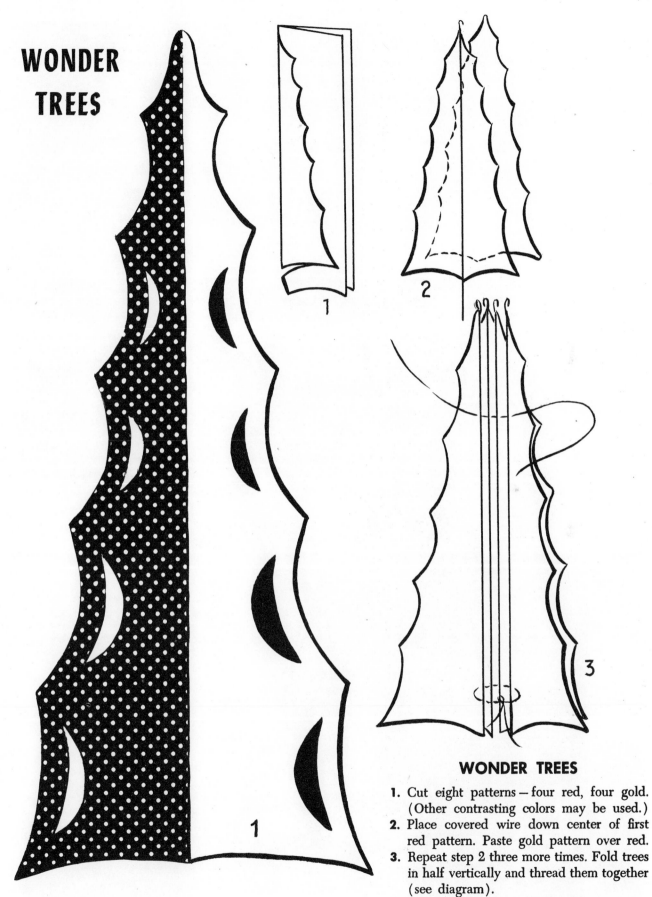

WONDER TREES

1. Cut eight patterns — four red, four gold. (Other contrasting colors may be used.)
2. Place covered wire down center of first red pattern. Paste gold pattern over red.
3. Repeat step 2 three more times. Fold trees in half vertically and thread them together (see diagram).
4. Use styrofoam base for support.

3-D tree made of
red enameled paper.

Wonder tree.

"WESOLYCH SWIAT"

THE "star of Bethlehem" sets the theme for Poland's Christmas traditions.

The first star in the evening sky on December 24 signals the end of the Christmas fast and the beginning of the Festival of the Star.

Straw is spread under the table in remembrance of the stable in Bethlehem and a chair is left vacant for the Holy Child.

Before the meal begins the tradition of the Peace Wafer is observed. The wafers are small, round, and flat, similar to those used in Communion. Previously blessed by the village priest, these wafers are distributed by the head of the family to all those around the table, with an exchange of good wishes. This symbolizes the peace and friendship of those present and comes from the ancient tradition of "breaking bread."

Following this simple ceremony dishes of mush, fish, and almonds are included in the meal. Token gifts, such as sugar hearts, cookies, or a silver coin are placed at each plate.

After supper the children are examined on their knowledge of religion by the Star Man (usually the village priest), after which they receive small gifts from the Wise Men, impersonated by three young men who carry a star and sing carols. The gifts are believed to come from the stars, with the Wise Men acting as emissaries.

It is customary for the young people in rural areas to accompany the Wise Men on their mission, dressed as animals or as characters from the Nativity scene symbolizing all those privileged to attend the Birth of the Christ Child. They go from house to house singing carols and are welcomed with a glass of wine and cookies. Some of the group may carry small stages for puppet shows which depict various biblical scenes or incidents.

Although the Polish Christmas tree may have many varieties of ornaments, and will differ in the city and in the country, stars in many varieties will be found on all. Red and white, the national colors, are popular in intricate paper decorations.

Heart-shaped ornaments are also used and much artistry is found in the various bird forms on the tree. The Polish royal crest is also used for decoration.

Polish customs through your hands.

111

PEASANT ANGEL

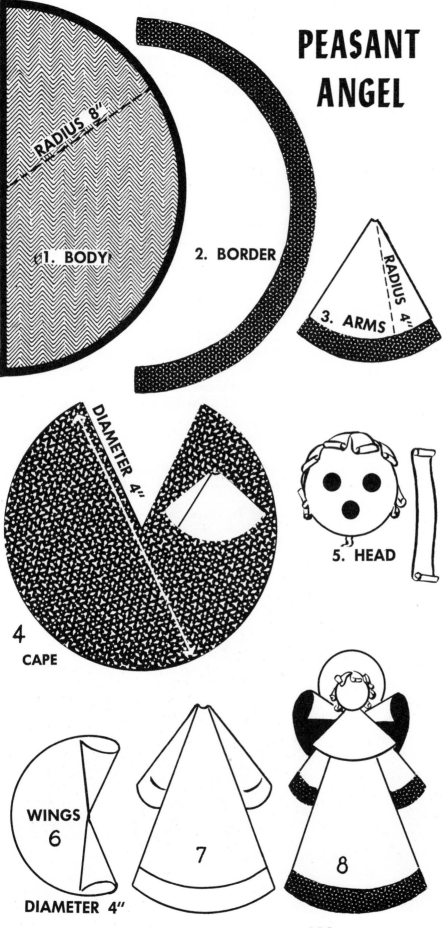

1. BODY

2. BORDER

3. ARMS — RADIUS 4"

RADIUS 8"

4 CAPE — DIAMETER 4"

5. HEAD

WINGS 6 — DIAMETER 4"

7

8

PEASANT ANGEL

1. For the body of the angel, make a semicircle with an 8-in. radius.

2. For the hem, cut a border from wallpaper or paint a design on any lightweight paper.

3. For the arms, use a 4-in. radius to make a circle. Divide circle into four or five segments. Use two of these segments for shaping arms.

4. For angel's cape, make a circle 4 in. in diameter. Shape it into a shallow cone.

5. For the head, use a wooden bead or Christmas ball. Paint features. For the hair, use narrow strips of paper; curl ends and glue to head.

6. For wings, make a circle 4 in. in diameter and cut in from any point on the circle toward the center. Turn down flaps as shown in Figure 6 and glue or staple in place.

7. Fasten arms to body of angel.

8. Attach cape over arms and insert head. Glue or staple wings to back of body and a paper halo to back of head.

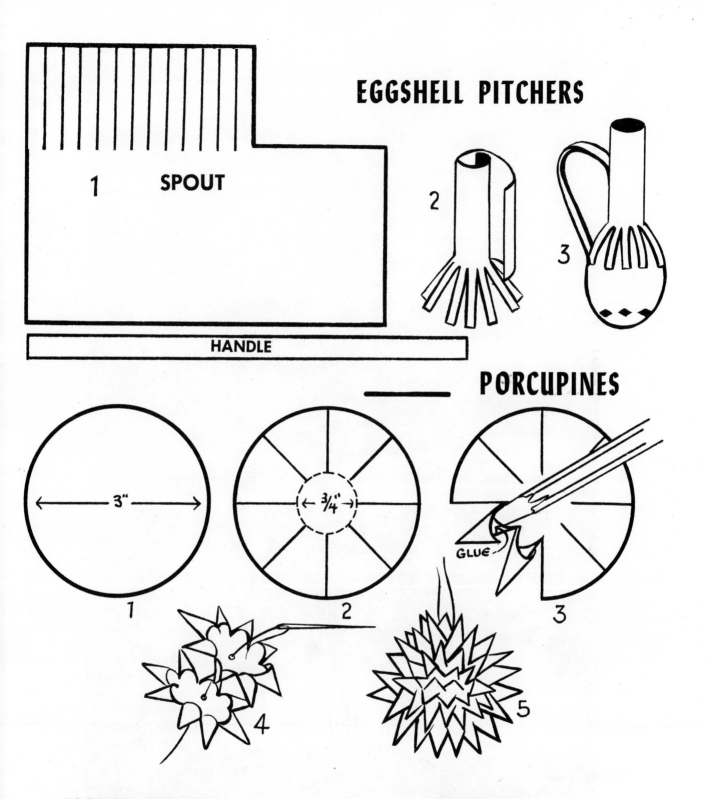

EGGSHELL PITCHERS

1 SPOUT

HANDLE

2

3

PORCUPINES

3"

¾"

GLUE

1

2

3

4

5

EGGSHELL PITCHER

1. Trace patterns of spout and handle.
2. Cut in on solid lines and roll into a cylinder. Glue tabs down on eggshell.
3. Attach handle to spout.

PORCUPINES

1. Make a circle 3 in. or more in diameter.
2. Within this circle draw another circle ¾ in. in diameter. Divide outer circle into eight parts as in Figure 2. Cut on lines as indicated.
3. Roll each part around point of pencil and glue flaps.
4. Make 12 such circles and string them as tightly as possible.
5. Tie and suspend.

Polish tree — symbol of peace and friendship.

Polish Designs

UKRAINE

"CHRYSTOS ROZDZAJETSIA SLAWYTE JEHO"

DURING the thirteenth century the Ukraine was controlled by the Kingdoms of Lithuania and of Poland, but since the seventeenth century, except for brief periods, it has been under the domination of Russia. Today the Ukraine is one of the sixteen constituents of the Union of Soviet Socialist Republics.

Thus its former Christian traditions are largely patterned on those of Lithuania and Poland, and its religious affiliation with the Eastern Church.

Christmas began with a forty-day fast, which ended on Christmas Eve with the appearance of the first star in the evening sky as the family sat down to a straw-covered table, to partake of the Christmas wafer. A twelve-course dinner followed, each course commemorating one of the twelve Apostles. Included were buckwheat and mushroom soup, pancakes in flax, cabbage, fish, prunes, a special Christmas bread, and nuts. A honey and porridge called *Koutia* was served to commemorate the Holy Crib. The porridge represented the straw in the manger and the honey, usually accompanied by fruit, symbolized the Infant.

During the meal, everyone was required to speak in low, sweet tones in order to obtain a blessing for the house — for peace, love, and affection were especially a part of this season.

Christmas was a three-day holiday devoted largely to visiting, singing, and dancing as well as to church services. Each day the Kolyadniky, or singing group, visited the homes in the village to sing the songs of Christmas and to partake of the refreshments offered by their hosts.

The priest also made his visits to bless each house and to examine the children in their catechism.

The agricultural life of the Ukraine and its limitations in finding future husbands prompted fortunetelling as a part of the season's customs. A young girl might find out what direction to look for her future husband by standing with her back to the gateway and kicking her party slipper into the air over her head. The direction the shoe pointed was the important feature, except when it pointed at the gate, in which case it meant she wouldn't get married — unless she decided to try again, of course.

Another method was to arrange two candles in front of two mirrors so that each candle was reflected in the other mirror. By looking hard, and counting each reflection, one's future lover could be seen in back of the seventh image.

One of the unusual ornaments of the Ukrainian tree is a spider and a web. It is considered lucky to find a spider web in the house on Christmas — although it might be pointed out that the spider who escapes the house-cleaning zeal of the Ukrainian housewife would be the lucky one. But the story goes that once a poor woman who was unable to provide any trimmings for the children's Christmas tree was surprised to find on Christmas morning that spiders had covered the tree with their webs during the night. When the first light of the Christmas morning sun struck the tree, the webs turned to silver.

Thus unexpected fortune was associated with finding a spider web on Christmas — and it was also a convenient way for the housewife to account for this apparent neglect of her duties.

But the artificial spider web on the tree insured good fortune in any event.

Nature's straw
yields itself into
man-made beauty.

CHEERY CHAIN

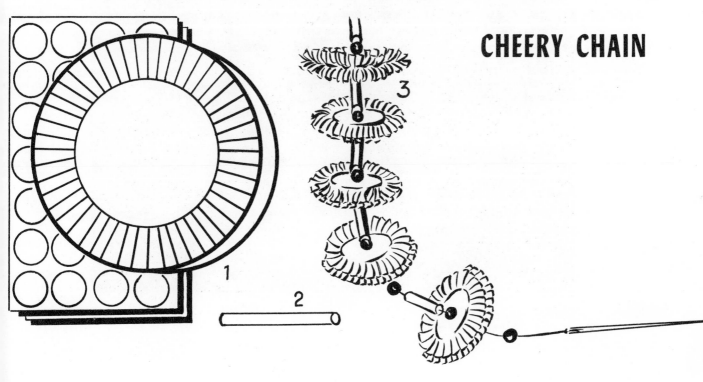

1

2

3

117

Ukrainian artistry.

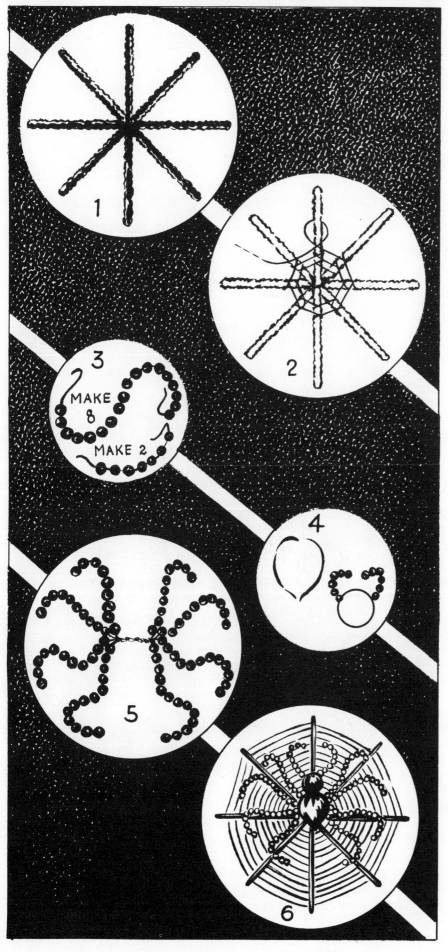

THE BEADED SPIDER

THE BEADED SPIDER

1. Cross four 8-in. pipe cleaners and reinforce at center with fine wire.
2. To form web, weave long string around pipe cleaners as shown in Figure 2.
3. For spider's leg, string small beads on a 4½-in. flexible wire. Make eight of these. String small beads on two pieces of wire each measuring 2½ in. to make antennae.
4. Insert the antennae into glittered styrofoam ball (head). For body, paint a half walnut shell in gold.
5. Wire legs together, four on each side.
6. Tie legs to web. Glue body and head to center of web.

CHEERY CHAIN

1. On the top sheet of several layers of tissue paper, trace and cut as many circles, 2 in. in diameter, as possible. Cut in toward center of circles, as shown.
2. Cut drinking straws into 1¼-in. segments.
3. Put two circles together and curl edges.
   String in this order:
   a) Two circles
   b) Bead
   c) Drinking straw
   d) Bead
   e) Repeat

RUSSIA

"S ROZHESTVÓM KHRISTÓVYM"

LITTLE remains today of old Christmas traditions in Russia. However, before the revolution, there were many interesting and colorful customs many of which antedated Christianity.

The appearance of the evening star on Christmas eve signaled the end of fasting and the *Colatzia*, or supper, was served on a straw-covered table. First the blessed wafer was divided among the family and friends to symbolize the peace and good will of the season. Following supper with its main dishes of fish and special cakes, the people joined in processions, wearing costumes representing the animals present in the stable at Bethlehem. They went through the village singing carols, many of which dated back to the old sacrificial songs of heathen days.

Church services were held at midnight and the next day was one of visiting friends and neighbors for party fun and dancing.

Foretelling the future at these parties involved various approaches. Melted wax or lead dropped in the snow took interesting forms which could be interpreted by the older women.

The younger women made five piles of grain on the kitchen floor, each pile signifying something for the future, such as wealth, marriage, hope, charcoal, and thread. A hen was brought in and whichever pile it went to first indicated the future of the girl involved. Charcoal meant death or illness for someone in the family, while thread indicated a life of toil.

The future could also be read in an egg yolk dropped into a glass of water. The following day its discolorations would reveal what lay ahead to those who could interpret properly.

In old Russia it was *Baboushka* who brought presents for good little boys and girls. Baboushka was believed to be a witchlike person who had misdirected the Wise Men on their way to Bethlehem. Now

her mission was to journey throughout the land, knocking on each door with her staff, seeking the Infant Child. While the children were asleep she would enter with a candle to look at them and then slip a toy under the pillow.

The Russian tree was decorated with iconlike images of the Virgin Mary and saints, along with birds and animals, nuts and candies.

Majestic towers and icons enhance the Russian tree.

COSSACK DOLL

BODY

COLLAR

HAT

ARMS

COSSACK DOLL

1. For body, cut out a semicircle having 5-in. radius. Use red construction or similar paper. Form semicircle into a cone. For head, insert a small Christmas or styrofoam ball into cone. Cut out collar and glue to body.
2. Bend pipe cleaner in half and fasten to back of body, just below head. Bring pipe cleaners forward and form arms. Roll arm patterns into cylinders and slip on to pipe cleaners. Make a wide tube for the muff. Form hat pattern into cone and glue to head.
3. Decorate doll with cotton.

LUMINOUS BIRD

TOWERS OF RUSSIA

LUMINOUS BIRD

1. Trace patterns of wings (A), tail (B), and head (C), using colored luminous paper.
2. Glue together as shown in diagram.

TOWERS OF RUSSIA

1. Cut a paper mailing tube (about 1½ in. in diameter) into 4-in. lengths.
2. Remove rim from a small water cup. Make slits around bottom of cup.
3. Glue cup to cylinder. Reinforce both by applying tape over slit parts. Sprinkle with glitter.

3-D ICON

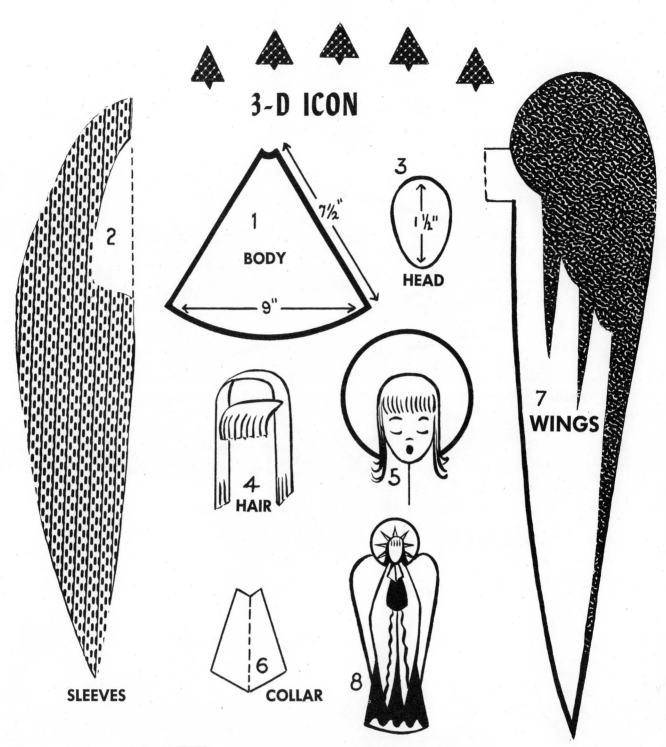

3-D ICONS

1. With a radius of 7½ in. make pattern of body from any colored, medium-weight paper. Shape into a cone.
2. Trace pattern of sleeves by placing the dotted side of pattern on folded edge of paper.
3. Form one 1½-in. oval head from styrofoam piece. Use sandpaper to obtain smooth surface.
4. For hair, cut paper strips to fit head.
5. Tape hair to head and paint features. Insert wire into head. Make wire long enough to fit into cone (body). Tape wire inside of cone. For halo, make a circle 2 in. in diameter on gold paper.
6. Trace pattern of collar and crease on dotted line.
7. Trace pattern of wings by placing tab with dotted lines on folded edge of paper.
8. Decorate pieces with glitter before assembling angel. Attach a halo to back of head. Paste collar, sleeves, and wings to body.

"KALA CHRISTOUGENA"

BREAD, water, and mischief might be said to be the principal characteristics of Christmas customs in Greece.

The bread is a special loaf, baked for the occasion, with a cross marked on top and a coin placed inside. First the house is incensed and then, as the family gathers about the table for the evening meal, the bread is broken into small pieces by the parents.

The first piece is put aside for St. Basil, an early "doctor of the Church," who is the patriarch of Eastern monks; or it may be for the Holy Virgin; or, as third alternative, for the patron saint of the family whose icon is kept in the house.

The second piece is intended for the house — that its occupants may be blessed spiritually and physically during the coming year. Next the farm animals receive a small portion that they too may share the blessings of the season. And the fourth piece symbolizes material possessions.

The remainder of this Christmas loaf is then divided among members of the family, beginning with the oldest. As each receives his portion it is dipped in wine and eaten with the words, "This is in remembrance of St. Basil, our blessed grandfather."

Good fortune and prosperity for the coming year is assured to the one who finds a coin in his bread portion. The coin itself is used to buy a candle for the church, to be lighted on Christmas day.

After the evening meal, the table is not cleared in the hope that St. Basil may share the repast.

The family now gathers about the fireplace for an evening of games, fortune-telling tricks, and storytelling.

One of the ancient customs reveals the future of young lovers. Two olive leaves, named for the boy and girl concerned, are placed on hot embers in the fire. As the heat shrivels the leaves, the way in which they curl indicates the course of love. If they curl toward each other, all is well. If they curl away, the couple will not be happy together. If, however, the leaves burst into flame immediately, the lovers are sure of the intensity of their affection and are promised a long life of marital bliss. The trick, for anyone who wants to insure the leaves behaving properly, is to pick a good hot part of the embers. And dry leaves help, too. These conditions could be reversed, if the maiden so desired.

The Christmas log must be kept burning all night and the fire itself is not allowed to go out until the Epiphany, to ward off the mischief-making exploits of mysterious beings — half human and half animal, known as the *Karkantzari*.

The *Karkantzari* wander about from Christmas to Epiphany and are especially fond of stirring up trouble for people who fall asleep after eating too well or too richly during the holidays. They account for all manner of trouble — indigestion, arguments with one's wife or sweetheart, mischief-making children, milk turning sour, horses and donkeys going lame, and any other misfortunes which may occur during the Christmas season. They may be kept under control by sprinkling holy water throughout the house, a ritual which the Orthodox Greek priest performs. Another good preventive measure is to burn old shoes in the fire during this time. Shoes are saved all during the year for this purpose, as it is believed the odor of burning leather keeps the creatures away.

 CONTINUED ON PAGE 128.

Greece sails on in
holiday fashion.

BOAT

1. Trace two boat patterns and one sail. Glue a contrasting strip to each side
of boat. Staple ends of two boat patterns together.

2. Insert a nut cup into boat and attach sail to cup.

ANGEL GARLAND

Cut a strip of paper about 1 yard long and 3½ in. wide. Pleat at 3½-in.
intervals. Trace angel on top pleat, having pattern touch both ends to insure an
unbroken chain. Cut out angel pattern.

GREECE

BOAT

1

2

GARLAND

ANGEL

3½"

3½"

127

Yuletide sails.

CONTINUED FROM PAGE 125.

Although no Christmas tree tradition was observed in Greece until the custom spread from others parts of Europe, the children received gifts from their patron, St. Basil. He is believed to make his rounds in a boat, which is proper in a country relying historically on the sea.

After Church services on Twelfth Day, Epiphany, the priests and people gather at a nearby river or spring for the ceremony of "Blessing the Waters." This is intended as a commemoration of Christ's baptism in the river Jordan, although it may also have antecedents in the pagan custom of honoring springs as part of the spring festival.

First, a white dove is released over the water as a symbol of the Holy Spirit. The priest then throws a cross into the water and the young men compete to recover it. A special blessing is always given to the successful one and there is great prestige attached to being thus honored.

Following this rite, the people fill containers with the water to be taken home and placed near their icons.

In many parts of the United States, where Greek communities are found, this tradition is still observed.

128

"SCHENORHAVOR DZENOUNT"

BOTH Christmas and New Year customs in Armenia are primarily religious in nature and do not take on the spirit of carnival that marks the traditions of so many other countries.

The week preceding Christmas is one of strict fasting, which comes to an end only after the Christmas Eve Communion. After returning home, all the house is illuminated with candles, and the evening meal is served.

Then the children gather in groups and going up to the housetops sing a song of rejoicing. They are rewarded with cookies, candy, fruit, and small coins.

The village priest visits the homes of his congregation where death has come during the year and says a special prayer for the souls of the departed.

It is customary for the young men to give their sweethearts special gifts at this time. These should include twelve pieces of cake (one for each month), a candle, some eggs, raisins and sweetmeats, and some perfumed cosmetics to indicate his ability to provide her with both the necessities and the luxuries of life.

Church services are held again on Christmas morning when water is blessed which will be used throughout the Christmas season for purification. At home it is mixed with earth and kept in a special bowl to be used for symbolical cleansing of dishes and other household objects.

There is much visiting during the next three days of the season, and many references to "happy blessing of the water" are exchanged.

The third day is especially set aside for the women to visit each other.

New Year's day is the time for all to visit their priest, with the men and women going in separate groups. After wishing him well for the coming year, they receive a special blessing and a piece of cake.

Similar visits are made by newly married bridegrooms to their parents-in-law. A gift of money is made to the mother-in-law, who in turn presents some article of wearing apparel.

A special dough is made for the New Year's visiting in the form of round, thick cakes with raisins and almonds. One piece of cake contains a coin that will bring good luck to the finder.

White doves proclaim the birth of the Prince of Peace.

130

FLIGHTS OF FANCY

STAR

FLIGHTS OF FANCY

Trace one pattern of bird and two patterns of wings. (Use white drawing paper.) Attach a wing to each side of body. Paint eyes on each side of bird pattern.

STAR

Cut sections from paper baking cups to make six-pointed stars. Glue two of them back to back. Secure centers with colored beads and suspend on branch.

CHINA

JAPAN

ALTHOUGH Christmas came to China and Japan from the Western world, national characteristics in both countries have made adaptations from the ancient traditions of the East.

Christmas in China is called *Sheng Dan Jieh* which means the Holy Birth Festival. The Christmas tree is called the "Tree of Light" and its decorations are usually paper chains, cotton snow, paper flowers and banners on which are inscribed Chinese characters meaning "peace" and "joy."

To lend a little more oriental atmosphere to our new look at a Chinese Christmas tree we have added a few symbols associated with this country. The ricksha model, for example, fashioned of paper and pipe cleaners makes an unusual tree ornament, or it may be used for a table centerpiece. And the butterflies and moths, which appear in many forms of Chinese art, are well suited for those who like their ornaments intricate and artistic. Simpler, but equally effective, are the paper silhouettes of ancient Chinese temples, and mobiles made to resemble Chinese kites. The traditional lanterns make shades to give even American Christmas tree lights an oriental appearance.

We have taken similar liberties with our Japanese ornaments, mixing modernized versions of Japanese folk motifs with traditional decorations.

The little wind chimes on our tree are found all over Japan, and especially in the temple grounds. They are made of small bits of glass or mirrors which tinkle in the slightest breeze to make a kind of faraway fairy music. Hanging on a Christmas tree, they reflect the lights and colors around them and enhance the touch of delicacy which makes the tree unusual. Little colored parasols and fans, made brilliant with metallic paper or sequins, are other ideas we have borrowed from Japanese ways for tree decorations.

Japanese cookies, made of rice flour, and known as *sembei*, are usually served with tea, but they can also be placed on the tree. It is customary in Japan to place in these cookies little slips of paper which contain printed messages of good fortune.

The carp is a fish held in high esteem in Japan, so our tree would not be complete without fish ornaments. We have also used little replicas of Shinto gates on our tree. In Japan, as one approaches the Shinto temples, the entrance is through such a gateway, which means "The Way of the Sacred." This is also the meaning of the word "Shinto," the Japanese state religion which is as old as Christianity. In our new-look-at-old-things approach to Christmas, its use as a tree ornament is simply a recognition of its artistic value, though some may prefer to find some other symbolical significance for it.

CHINESE PAGODAS
3-D PAGODA

Make two pagoda patterns. Fold each pattern on dotted line and glue together to form a four-sided ornament. Decorate with beads (Fig. 2).

BOX PAGODA

1. Trace pattern of roof and fold on dotted lines.
2. Make wall of pagoda by following indicated sizes in Figure 2. Fold on dotted lines. Glue ends together to form a rectangular box (Fig. 4).
3. Glue doors to sides of pagoda.
4. Tape roof to box.
5. Suspend beads from eaves of roof (Fig. 5).

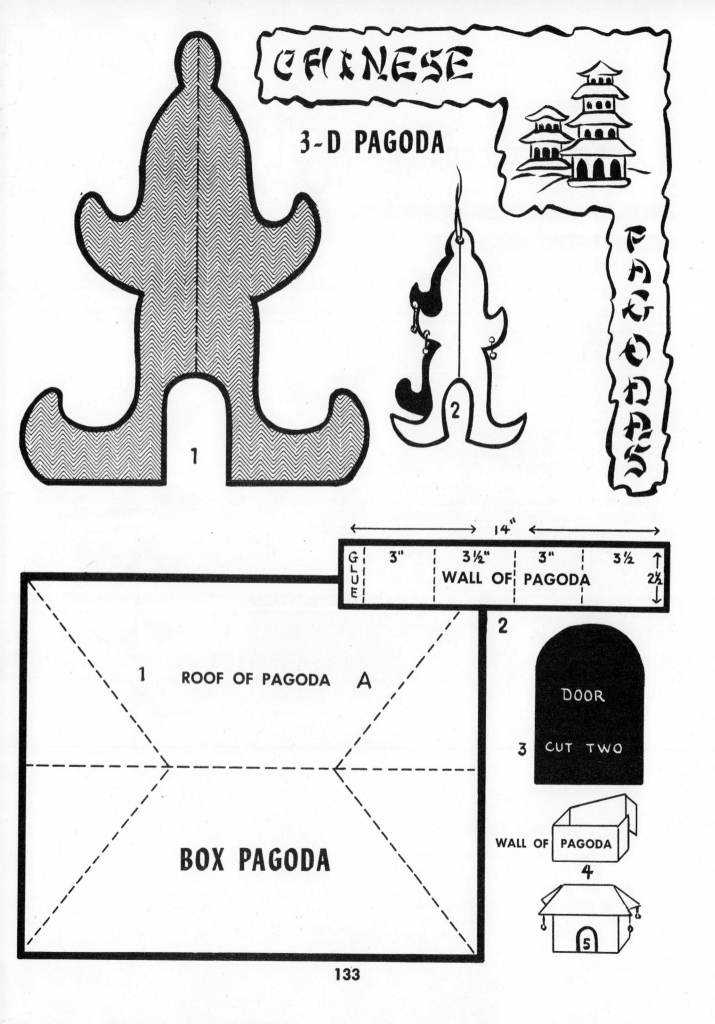

CHINESE

3-D PAGODA

PAGODAS

1

2

GLUE	3"	3½" WALL OF PAGODA	3"	3½

14"

2½

2

1 ROOF OF PAGODA A

DOOR

3 CUT TWO

WALL OF PAGODA

4

BOX PAGODA

5

AIRBORNE PAGODA

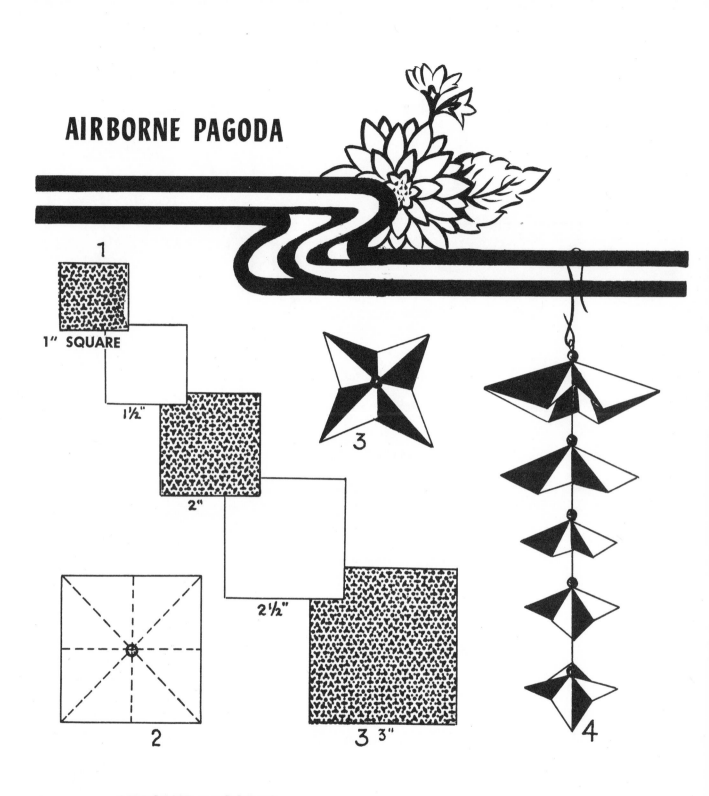

1 1" SQUARE

1½"

2"

2½"

2

3

3 3"

4

AIRBORNE PAGODAS

1–3. Fold each of five squares on dotted lines as shown in Figure 2. (Fold diagonals up and short lines down.)

4. String parts together beginning with smallest piece, using colored beads on top of each folded square. Tie knot after 2-in. intervals to keep beads and squares from sliding.

JINRIKISHA

JINRIKISHA

Trace and cut one seat, two sides, and two wheels from heavy gold paper. Fold seat on dotted lines and tape to sides of jinrikisha (Fig. A). Fasten wheels on either side. Decorate both sides with glitter. Tape two long pipe cleaners to sides to serve as pulleys.

135

Pagodas on parade.

Chinese tree of light.

Jinrikisha in gold.

ORIENTAL BUTTERFLY

ORIENTAL BUTTERFLY

1. Trace butterfly pattern from colored mat stock. Use black construction paper for dark areas of butterfly.

2–3. Glue colorful feathers to wings.

137

JAPAN

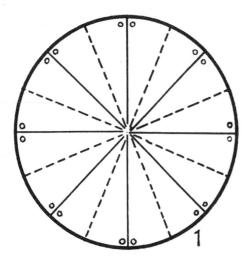

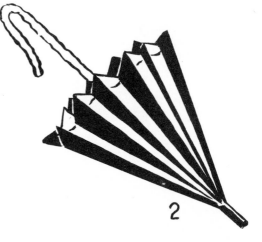

UMBRELLA

1. Divide a circle measuring 8 in. in diameter into sixteen parts. Use colored construction paper. Fold outwardly on heavy lines and inwardly on dotted lines. Punch holes as shown in Figure 1, then draw heavy colored string or ribbon through holes (Fig. 1).
2. For handle, fasten pipe cleaner to center of umbrella with tape. Make a loop at the top of handle large enough to suspend on tree branch (Fig. 2).

STORK PATTERN

Trace patterns of head, tail, and wings from any foil paper.
1. Curl the narrow, pointed end of head (Fig. 1).
2. Shape tail pattern into a cone (Fig. 2).
3. Fold wing pattern on dotted lines to form body and wings (Fig. 3). Shape wings with any dull metal instrument.
4. Attach head and tail to body with tape.

138

Foil fanfare.

JAPAN

Japanese
splendor.

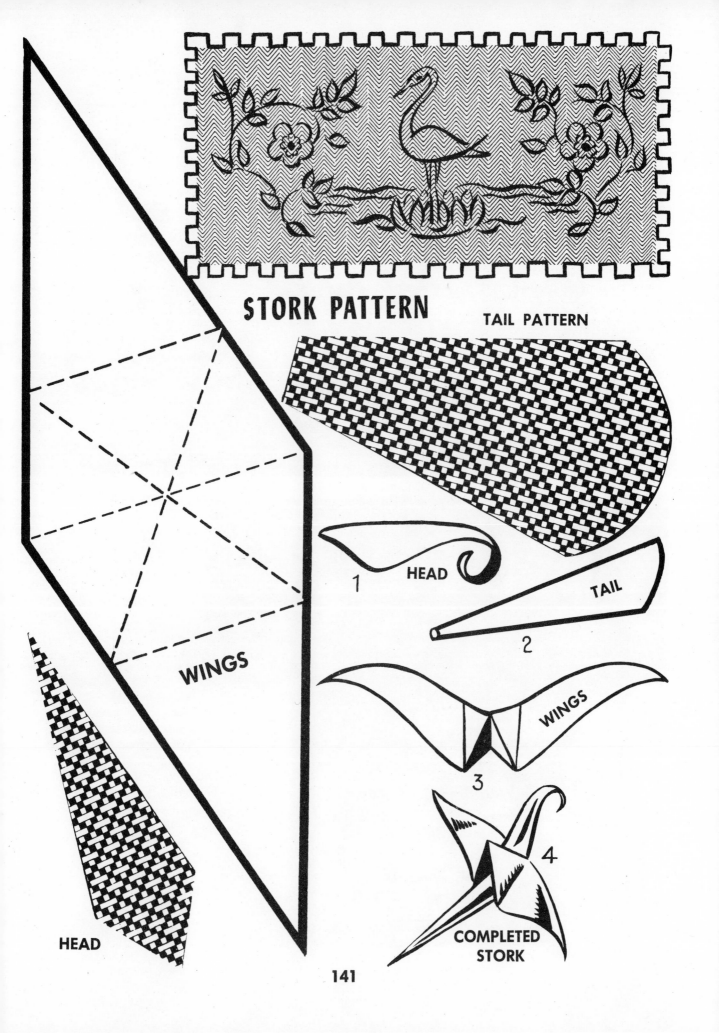

STORK PATTERN

TAIL PATTERN

1 HEAD

2 TAIL

3 WINGS

WINGS

HEAD

4

COMPLETED
STORK

141

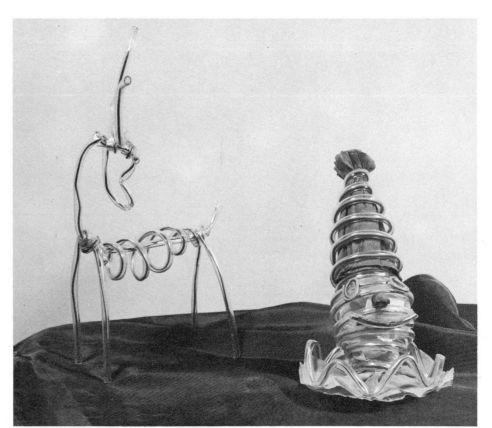

Discarded polyethylene
tubing and wire produce
unusual effects.

Scrap sheet metal
successfully used with
polyethylene tubing.

Pine-cone and
pipe-cleaner
combination.

Madonna backed with palms.

Angel in Gothic setting.

A sheet of wallpaper and a dash of ingenuity will wrap
an elegant package.

REFERENCE SOURCES

A. Books

Baltrusaitis, Jurgis, *Lithuanian Folk Art*, J. G. Weiss'sche Buch Druckerei, Munich, Germany, 1948.

Betts, V. B., *Exploring Papier-Mâché*, Davis Press, Inc., Worcester, Mass., 1955.

Cereghini, Mario, *Architecture in The Alps*, Milan, Italy, 1953.

Dmytriw, Olya, *Ukrainian Arts*, Ukrainian Youth's League of North America, Inc., New York, N. Y., 1955.

Doten, H. R., and Boulard, C., *Fashion Drawing*, Harper and Bros., New York, N. Y., 1939.

Encisco, Jorge, *Design Motifs of Ancient Mexico*, Dover, Inc., New York, N. Y., 1953.

Estrin, Michael, *2000 Designs, Forms and Ornaments*, Wm. Penn Publishing Company, New York, N. Y., 1947.

Evans, Mary, A.M., *Costume Throughout The Ages*, J. B. Lippincott Co., Chicago, Ill., 1938.

Galaune, Paulius, *Lithuanian Folk Art*, J. Karvelis, Chicago, Ill., 1956.

Gardner, Horace J., *Let's Celebrate Christmas*, A. S. Barnes and Co., New York, N. Y., 1940.

Halfdan, Arneberg, *Norwegian Peasant Art*, Fabritius and Sonner, Oslo, Norway, 1949.

Hallen, Julienne, *Folk Art Design*, Homecrafts, New York, N. Y., 1949.

Hauglid, Roar, *Norway, A Thousand Years of Native Arts and Crafts*, Mittet & Co., Oslo, Norway, 1956.

―――― *Native Arts of Norway*, Mittet & Co., Oslo, Norway, 1953.

Hercik, Emanuel, *Folk Toys*, Orbis, Prague, Czechoslovakia, 1952.

Lederer, Charlotte, *Made in Hungary*, Dr. George Wajna & Co., Budapest, Hungary.

Lester, Katherine M., *Historic Costume*, Chas. A. Bennett Co., Inc., Peoria, Ill., 1956.

Mann, Kathleen, *Design from Peasant Art*, Adam and Charles Black, London, England, 1939.

Meyer, Franz S., *Handbook of Ornament*, Dover, Inc., New York, N. Y., 1957.

Piotrowska, Irena, *The Art of Poland*, Philosophical Library, Inc., New York, N. Y., 1947.

Plath, Iona, *The Decorative Arts of Sweden*, Chas. Scribner's Sons, New York, N. Y., 1948.

Popular Mechanics Press, Chicago, Ill., *Christmas Handbook*, 1932.

Rice, Tamara Talbot, *Russian Art*, Richard Clay and Co., Bungay, Suffolk, 1949.

Schauffler, Grace L., *How to Make Your Own Dolls*, Hobby Book Mart, New York, N. Y., 1948.

Snead, Jane, *Chinese Designs*, Jane Snead, Media, Pa., 1950.

Speltz, Alexander, *Styles of Ornament*, Grosset and Dunlap, New York, N. Y.

Stewart, Janice, *The Folk Arts of Norway*, University of Wisconsin Press, Madison, Wis., 1953.

Then, John N., *Christmas Comes Again*, The Bruce Publishing Co., Milwaukee 1, Wis., 1939.

Toor, Frances, *Mexican Popular Arts*, McBride and Co., Manchester, Mexico, 1939.

Tsuda, Noritake, *Handbook of Japanese Art*, Sanseido Co., Ltd., Tokyo, Japan, 1936.

Voyce, Arthur, *Russian Architecture*, Philosophical Library, New York, N. Y., 1948.

Weiser, Rev. Francis X., S.J., *Religious Customs in the Family*, The Liturgical Press, Collegeville, Minn., 1956.

―――― *The Christmas Book*, Harcourt, Brace and Co., New York, N. Y., 1952.

B. Pamphlets, Brochures

Austrian Information Service
31 East 69th St.
New York 21, N. Y.

British Travel Association
336 Madison Ave.
New York 17, N. Y.

Consulate General of Finland
Finland House
41 East 50th St.
New York 22, N. Y.

Danish Information Service
588 Fifth Ave.
New York 36, N. Y.

Finnish National Travel Office
41 East 50th St.
New York 22, N. Y.

French Cultural Services
972 Fifth Ave.
New York 21, N. Y.

German Tourist Information Service
500 Fifth Ave.
New York 36, N. Y.

Irish Tourist Information Bureau
33 East 50th St.
New York 22, N. Y.

Italian State Tourist Office
21 East 51st St.
New York 22, N. Y.

Lithuanian Consulate
6147 S. Artesian Ave.
Chicago 29, Ill.

Netherlands Information Service
10 Rockefeller Plaza
New York 20, N. Y.

Norwegian Information Service
Norway House
290 Madison Ave.
New York 17, N. Y.

Official Belgian Tourist Bureau
589 Fifth Ave.
New York 17, N. Y.

Swedish National Travel Office
630 Fifth Ave.
New York 20, N. Y.

Swiss National Travel Office
Rockefeller Plaza
10 West 49th St.
New York, N. Y.

Yugoslav Information Center
816 Fifth Ave.
New York 21, N. Y.

MATERIALS FOR CHRISTMAS DECORATIONS

The following supplies may be obtained from your local art supply store.

PAPERS

CELLOPHANE — Transparent, glassy paper. Comes in a variety of colors.

COLORED CONSTRUCTION PAPER — Suitable for crayon and tempera painting.

FINGER-PAINT PAPER — Coated on one side to take finger paints properly.

FLAMEPROOF CREPE PAPER — Chemically treated to resist fire and flame. Used for displays and decorations.

FLUORESCENT OR LUMINOUS PAPER — Bright coated paper with startling brilliance and color.

HIGHLY COATED AND VERY BRIGHTLY COLORED PAPERS — Excellent where bright accents are needed.

MAT STOCK — Dull-textured paper used for construction work. Comes in a variety of colors.

NEWSPAPER — Toy animals are made by adding layers of newspapers and paste over wire forms.

SHELF PAPER — Desirable for three-dimensional ornaments. Comes in all colors.

VELOUR PAPER — Has a velvetlike surface. Used for many decorative purposes.

WHITE DRAWING PAPER — Comes in different weights. The 70 lb. and 80 lb. are recommended for construction work.

FOIL PAPERS

ALUMINUM FOIL — Heavy and easy to handle. Excellent for tree ornaments.

COLORED METAL-FOIL PAPERS — Papers backed with genuine metal foil. Used for flakes, bells, garlands, and favors.

HEAVY-DUTY METALLIC PAPER — Excellent for constructing figures.

PAINTS

CASEIN COLORS — Casein paints can be used on any absorbent painting surface. Permanent and brilliant. Quick-drying colors completely intermixable with each other.

FINGER PAINT — Can easily be made from powder paint mixed with paste or liquid starch.

FLUORESCENT SHOWCARD PAINTS — Glow in broad daylight and give vivid effects that cannot be achieved by other paints.

LIQUID TEMPERA — Opaque colors come in jars and cover all surfaces. Finely ground and smooth.

LIQUID WHITE SHOE POLISH — Quick, easy, and inexpensive for light snow effects.

OIL PAINT — Made as follows:
1. Dissolve two tablespoons of tempera powder with a little turpentine, making a thick paste.
2. Add three tablespoons of varnish. Stir until smooth.

OIL STICK — An oil paint in stick form. One may obtain a wide variety of techniques ranging from brilliant crayon textures to painting effects. Works well on rough-textured paper.

TEMPERA DYE — Sawdust can be dyed with thinned tempera colors.

TEMPERA SPATTER WORK — Use toothbrush or spray gun. Be sure to thin tempera paint with water. Snow and winter effects obtained from spatter work.

TEMPERA SPONGE WORK — Variety of textures may be obtained by applying paint with a sponge. Beautiful gift wrapping papers can be made from ordinary shelf paper.

TEMPERA-TINTED SOAP — Ornaments dipped in tempera-tinted soap powder and starch combination give a frosted appearance.

THICK TEMPERA — May be used in dry brush stippling. Use stiff bristle brush to obtain best results.

TRANSPARENT WATER COLORS — Clean blending of colors. Paper seen through washes.

BRONZE PAINTS

ALUMINUM BRONZE — Mixed with bronzing liquid. Will resemble silver leaf.

GOLD OR SILVER POWDER — Used for gilding plant material. Mix powder with bronzing liquid and apply with brush. Powders may be obtained in the following shades: pale gold, deep gold, bright gold, copper, aluminum. (Gold or silver spray is commonly used today.)

SPRAYS AND SNOW EFFECTS

ARTIFICIAL SNOW — May be sprinkled on evergreens which have been brushed over with quick drying shellac.

DIAMOND DUST — Produces snow effects on cards, displays, ornaments, etc.

LACQUER SPRAY — Enamels and lacquers are made similar to oil paint. Add more varnish to obtain glossy effect. Apply two or three coats. Sandpaper after each coat.

LUMINOUS OR FLUORESCENT SPRAY PAINTS — Have an unusual brilliancy and sparkle. To be used on any white surface of paper, wood, glass, or metal.

FROTHY SNOW EFFECTS — Mix one cup of soap flakes with half cup of water and beat the mixture with a fork or egg beater until it is the consistency of whipped cream. Dip paint brush into mixture and apply lightly to branch.

PLASTIC SNOW SPRAY — A white spray that resembles glistening snow. Used for displays, ornaments, trees, etc.

PLASTIC SPRAY — Forms a clear permanent coating. Preserves and beautifies on one application. Branches, ferns, leaves, etc., are preserved with plastic spray.

CHALKS, CRAYONS, PENCILS

CHALK PASTELS — Compressed chalk.

CRAYONS — For drawing on wood, paper, fabric. Strong, brilliant, and easy to handle.

COLORED DRAWING PENCILS — Moistureproof, permanent, and strong, heavy leads.

MISCELLANEOUS SUPPLIES

FLORAL CLAY — Used to anchor materials.

FLORISTS' THREAD — Heavily waxed thread ideal for wreath-making.

GLITTER — Bright metallic particles which reflect light. Used for display, ornaments, favors, etc.

PLASTIC FOAM — (Styrofoam) Bought in blocks. Ideal for many types of holiday decorations.

WATERPROOF INKS — Soluble and waterproof. Used for fine line work and washes. Comes in many colors.

ADHERENTS

Glue
Household cement
Library paste (least expensive)
Paper cement

FASTENERS

Eyelets
Gummed paper
Paper clips
Paper fasteners (may be used as hooks for ornaments)
Stapler tacker
Straight pins (most versatile, inexpensive)

TAPES

Drafting tape — Holds paper or cloth to cardboard.
Masking tape — Used for all purposes.
Transparent cellophane adhesive tape.

DISCARDED MATERIAL

TYPES	SOURCES

PAPER

Trade-mark leavings, sample books, gift wrappings, Crepe paper, sample rolls and books of wallpaper, discarded Christmas cards, facial tissues, glazed shelf paper, doilies. — Manufacturers of paper, binderies, publishers and printers of advertising material, kitchens.

Cellophane. — Manufacturers of cellophane, package wrappings of all kinds, cellophane straws.

CUPS — drinking, ice cream, baking, souffle; pie plates and other paper containers. — Manufacturers of paper cups (discarded).

CARDBOARD — scraps, sheets, boxes (square, rectangular). — Cereal, cooky, and milk cartons; candy, cereal, match, dress and shoe boxes.

Cardboard boxes (round). — Hat boxes, ice cream, cosmetic, cheese, preserve, oatmeal, salt, and art supply containers.

Cardboard tubes. — Manufacturers of cardboard tubes, paper roll, cigar, mailing, paper towel, toilet tissue, and yard good tubes.

Corrugated cardboard boxes and containers. — Containers used in packing and shipping, school supplies, canned goods, wearing apparel, and all kinds of food, etc.

WOOD

Sawdust and pencil shavings, dowel rod wastes, small pieces of wood, florist's sticks. — Lumber yards, carpenter shops, manufacturers of furniture and store fixtures, and cabinetmakers.

Wooden spools — Manufacturers of rugs, cloth, thread, yarn, etc., dressmakers, and tailors.

Ice cream and lollipop sticks, spoons, tongue depressors, tooth picks, used matches, clothes pins, wooden beads, buttons, curtain rings. — Restaurants, school cafeterias, hospitals, household wastes.

Wooden baskets and crates (thin wood). — Vegetable and fruit packers.

FABRICS

Ravels, sample goods, old clothes, curtains, table coverings, buckram, tarlaton, and ribbon. — Manufacturers, tailors, dressmakers, wholesale houses.

FELT AND WOOL

Scraps, men's hats, women's bags, belts, jackets, pennants, etc. — Manufacturers, wholesale houses, discarded apparel.

Sweaters, mittens, socks, hats, scarves or stoles, and toys. — Discarded articles found in the home.

TWINE

Package wrapping string and rope, assorted samples of thread, yarn and twine, braided cord. — Samples from manufacturers, department stores, and household wastes.

TYPES	SOURCES

METAL AND FOIL

Metal strappings, tin and wire, cans (round and square), bottle tops, coat hangers, and copper screening.	Used in strapping bales of cotton, magazines, paper, and for shipping cartons, fruit and vegetable cans, tobacco, candy, cigar cans, trays, screens, etc.
Foil	Manufacturers of foil, food wrappings, candy, pastry, and tea wrappings.

MISCELLANEOUS

Cork, styrofoam, sandpaper, beads (all kinds), candles, plaster, braiding, egg crate dividers, cotton, broken colored glass, polyethelyne tubing, clinkers, etc.	Manufacturers, carpenter shops, household wastes, back yards, farms, hospitals, grocers, etc.

MATERIALS FROM NATURE

Branches, twigs, reed, bark of trees, driftwood, moss, fungus, dried grasses, wheat straw, milkweed pods, various weeds, corn husks, fern, gourds.	Centerpieces, window displays, party favors, ornaments, tree trimmings, backgrounds, etc.
Pine cones, acorns, nuts, peanuts, seeds (squash, pumpkin, corn kernels, sunflower, etc.).	Used for tree trimmings, centerpieces, pins, lapel ornaments (seeds used to make garlands in decorating tree).
Sand, sea shells, pebbles, stones, fish scales, etc.	Diorama construction.
Eggshells, feathers, butterflies, etc.	Tree trimmings.